DEACON BOOKS

What Does Christ Want?

GEOFFREY CHAPMAN

LONDON   DUBLIN   MELBOURNE   1968

WHAT DOES CHRIST WANT ?

Bernard Häring, C.Ss.R.

Geoffrey Chapman Ltd
18 High Street, Wimbledon, London SW 19

Geoffrey Chapman (Ireland) Ltd
5–7 Main Street, Blackrock, County Dublin

Geoffrey Chapman Pty Ltd
44 Latrobe Street, Melbourne, Vic 3000, Australia

First published 1968

Nihil Obstat:
  Edward J. Montano, S.T.D.
  Censor Librorum

Imprimatur:
  Terence J. Cooke, D.D.
  Auxiliary Bishop of N.Y.
New York, N.Y. – January 9, 1968

Made and Printed in Great Britain by
Fletcher & Son Ltd, Norwich

Acknowledgments

Some of the chapters in this book were reproduced with permission during 1967 in *Ave Maria* magazine. My intention, then as now, was to give an integrated perspective on Christian morality in such a way that others besides those trained in school theology should be able to profit. I kept all intelligent Christians in mind.

I want to express my gratitude to the translator, Mr. Albert Wimmer and to my sister, Sr. Lucidia Häring as well as to Sr. Jean Gabrielle and Mrs. Josephine McDonald Ryan who helped me in the final revision of the English text.

March 1968
Bernard Häring, C.Ss.R.

CONTENTS

Acknowledgments — 5

Introduction — 11

CHAPTER ONE
THE SERMON ON THE MOUNT — 15

CHAPTER TWO
GOOD NEWS AND THE COMMANDMENTS — 25

CHAPTER THREE
THE COMMANDMENT OF LOVE — 35

CHAPTER FOUR
THE SERMON ON THE MOUNT AND
THE FIRST TABLE OF THE DECALOGUE — 45

CHAPTER FIVE
THE SERMON ON THE MOUNT AND
THE SECOND COMMANDMENT — 53

CHAPTER SIX
THE SABBATH WAS MADE FOR MAN — 63

CHAPTER SEVEN
SACRAMENTS AND THE FORMATION OF LIFE — 71

CHAPTER EIGHT
LOVE OF NEIGHBOR AND
EXPRESSION OF NEIGHBORLY LOVE — 81

CHAPTER NINE
THE COMING OF AGE OF NEIGHBORLY LOVE — 93

CHAPTER TEN
THE PERSON IN COMMUNITY AND SOCIETY — 105

CHAPTER ELEVEN
WE ARE THE CHURCH — 117

CHAPTER TWELVE
THE CHRISTIAN IN MARRIAGE AND FAMILY — 129

CHAPTER THIRTEEN
RESPONSIBLE PARENTHOOD — 139

CHAPTER FOURTEEN
FAMILY RELATIONSHIPS — 155

CHAPTER FIFTEEN
CELIBACY FOR THE SAKE OF
THE KINGDOM OF HEAVEN — 167

CHAPTER SIXTEEN
CONVERSION TO ECUMENICAL
THINKING AND ACTING — 179

CHAPTER SEVENTEEN
BLESSED ARE THE PEACEMAKERS — 193

CHAPTER EIGHTEEN
MAN — THE PRODUCT OR THE
SHAPER OF HIS ENVIRONMENT? — 203

CHAPTER NINETEEN
WITNESSES TO TRUTH — 213

CHAPTER TWENTY
ESCHATOLOGICAL AND TIMELY VIRTUES — 223

How happy are the poor in spirit:
  theirs is the kingdom of heaven.

Happy the gentle:
  they shall have the earth for their heritage.

Happy those who mourn:
  they shall be comforted.

Happy those who hunger and thirst for what is right:
  they shall be satisfied.

Happy the merciful:
  they shall have mercy shown them.

Happy the pure in heart:
  they shall see God.

Happy the peacemakers:
  they shall be called sons of God.

Happy those who are persecuted in the cause of right:
  theirs is the kingdom of heaven.

Introduction

In this series of articles on "What Does Christ Want?" I would like to take my readers to the mountain of the beatitudes and into the room of the Last Supper. There we want to look at our Lord, listen to His words, and meditate on His "Happy are you." Through the "Good News" addressed to us, we shall try to understand what the Lord expects of us here and today. He is the giver of our law: He is the way, the truth and the life.

Let us forget for a while all our daily cares so as to listen intently to the Good News and the moral message of the Lord. Soon we will realize, however, that there is room for the images of our daily life in the clear air on the mountain of the beatitudes. For the Lord takes us infinitely seriously *just as we are* as soon as we take Him seriously for His own sake. He has a message for us which sheds light on our questions about life and on our sphere of existence: "You are the light of the world" (Mt. 5:14).

The chapters in this book are intended to be a contribution toward the postconciliar renewal of our lives. It requires that we totally surrender to the spirit of the Gospel, so that we may face our world with the right spirit and thus bring salvation to it; it also implies that we listen to the "signs of the times," which we can interpret only to the extent that we look and listen to Christ who makes the Good News of the heavenly kingdom known to us.

When Christianity was still the axis of our culture—and faith was still accepted unquestioningly as the norm for our thought and deeds—it was less harmful to summarize the bare commandments and duties of Christians in catechism and sermons, in education and in spiritual guidance without having to point constantly to the fundamentals of faith.

Today the situation is different. We are living in a world where a variety of ideologies and philosophies of life also produce differences in moral concepts. As Christians we have to become more aware of what it means to be a Christian if we are to avoid simple assimilation of ourselves to the *Zeitgeist* (spirit of the age). We must be in a position to justify our faith and the foundation of our morality to ourselves and to our neighbors and fellow citizens. This must be complemented by honest ecumenical concern. We Christians must all be equally at home in the world of Holy Scripture, the basis for a better understanding of one another, so that together we may make known and witness to the world our Lord, Jesus Christ, and His moral message.

The following presentation of Christian morality does not take the Ten Commandments of the law of the Old Covenant as its point of departure. The center of our Christian life is *Christ*. We must first listen to His sermon as handed down to us by the inspired authors of the New Testament. The place of the Old Testament's Sinai law— the Ten Commandments—is of secondary importance in a truly Christian approach. It will become clear to every reader that it is impossible to simply ignore the Ten Commandments; but we should not consider them only in their imperfect Old Testament form. That which was present in a hidden way in the Old Testament does not become completely known until the New Covenant. The moral teaching of the New Testament is of a beauty which, in comparison to the Decalogue, could not have been envisioned prior to it.

In keeping with the tradition of Catholic moral theology we shall also speak of commandments and virtues. But the decisive angle shall be the Sermon on the Mount (Mt. 5-7) and the farewell discourses of Jesus (Jn. 13-17). This will show us that there is more to Christian life than just commandments and virtues. But at the same time both commandments and virtues will appear all the more lovable and obligatory the more they appear in the light of the "Good News."

Is the Sermon on the Mount merely a collection of pious admonitions without any obligation? Or does it offer us detailed solutions to concrete questions which we can apply, without too much trouble, to our own life? Does it give us legal directives valid for all times and places? Answers to such questions are of fundamental importance to the understanding of Christian morals.

CHAPTER ONE

The Sermon on the Mount

The entire structure of the "Sermon on the Mount" and the literary form used by the Evangelist Matthew clearly and explicitly show that St. Matthew, following the intent of the Lord, wants to contrast the New Law with the Law of the Old Testament as the Old Law's fulfillment.

Expression of the New Law

Since Matthew wrote his Gospel for the Jewish Christians, we must bear in mind the common knowledge of his readers. When he mentioned the manifestation of the divine will on the Mount, they all recalled Mount Sinai hidden by flames and smoke, illuminated by lightning, vibrating with thunder, while Moses, on top of the mountain, received the Law of the Covenant. "Yahweh said to Moses, 'I am coming to you in a dense cloud so that the people may hear when I speak to you and may trust you always. . . . Go to the people and tell them to prepare themselves today and tomorrow. Let them wash their clothes and hold themselves in readiness for the third day, because on the third day Yahweh will descend on the mountain of Sinai in the sight of all the people. You will mark out the limits of the mountain and say, "Take care not to go up the mountain or to touch the foot of it. Whoever touches the mountain will be put to death. No one must lay hand on him: he must be stoned or shot down by arrow, whether man or

beast; he must not remain alive" ' " (Ex. 19:9-13). "Yahweh
came down on the mountain of Sinai, on the mountain top,
and Yahweh called Moses to the top of the mountain; and
Moses went up. Yahweh said to Moses, 'Go down and
warn the people not to pass beyond their bounds to come
and look on Yahweh, or many of them will lose their lives' "
(Ex 19:20-22; cf Ex 34:1-3).

In contrast to this revelation of God, which reflected the
hardheartedness of the Jewish people at the time of Moses
and which correspondingly emphasized God's awesome
holiness and sublime nature, the Sermon on the Mount
clearly accentuates the comforting truth of the Emmanuel—
God with us. "The kingdom of heaven is close at hand"
(Mt 4:17). Jesus invites His friends to imitate Him most
intimately by calling everyone by name. "Follow me"
(Mt 4:19).

Luke's shorter wording of the Sermon on the Mount
(Lk 6:17-49) is introduced by the selection of the twelve
Apostles. Jesus prayed in seclusion on the mountain throughout the night. Then He summoned His disciples and
selected twelve from among them. "He then came down
with them and took his stand on level ground" (Lk 6:17).

Both Gospels emphasize that Jesus pronounces His
teachings and His commandment in the presence of all of
His disciples and a large gathering of the people. "There
was a large gathering of his disciples with a great crowd of
people from all parts of Judaea and from Jerusalem and
from the coastal region of Tyre and Sidon who had come
to hear him and to be cured of their diseases" (Lk 6:17-18).
The reference to the inhabitants from the regions of Tyre
and Sidon is found in Luke only, he interpreted the Sermon
on the Mount for the benefit of the heaten and the Christians among them. He mentions Tyre and Sidon because

he wanted to stress the universality of the teachings of Jesus with respect to these people.

However, the Gospels of both Matthew and Luke make the strikingly clear contrast with Mount Sinai which was forbidden to the people. It is the Good News of the miraculous condescension of God through His incarnation. Luke expresses this figuratively through the summoning of the Apostles on the mountain of prayer and through the descent to the plain on which Jesus joins the crowd.

Matthew speaks of the ascent to the mountain in order to point out to the Jewish Christians the true mountain of the New Law and the sublime nature of the calling. At the same time, however, he wants to show how this lofty calling is addressed to everybody: "Seeing the crowds, he went up the hill. There he sat down and his disciples gathered around him. Then he began to speak" (Mt 5:12). Here the proximity of "God with us" and the authority with which He solemnly teaches appear in a stirring synthesis.

In his magnificent picture of the moral message of Jesus, St. John expresses the same truth in a different manner. He presents Jesus at the Last Supper. In anticipation of the Easter mystery of death and resurrection and with respect to the institution of the Holy Eucharist, Jesus announces His New Law to everybody who receives life from and through Him. Just as He institutes the Eucharist for all men, the New Law applies to everybody. He teaches with absolute authority, but it is exactly through His presence that He teaches: "You call me Master and Lord, and rightly; so I am" (Jn 13:12). In the Sermon on the Mount the first beatitude and the first commandment is gentleness— poverty. The washing of the feet, the most humble service, appears in the Gospel of St. John as both example and teaching—a blessed command. It is God's inscrutable condescension, the gentleness of the Incarnate Word, which constitutes proximity and thus teaches and instructs with authority.

Jesus Teaches with Authority

The great teachers of the law after Moses explained the Decalogue, surrounded it with bylaws and partially rephrased it so that it remained intelligible to new generations. The teaching of Jesus as summed up in the Sermon on the Mount goes far beyond a mere interpretation of the law. He teaches in His own right. He is more than Moses. He brings everything to fulfillment. "Do not imagine that I have come to abolish the Law or the Prophets. I have come not to abolish them but to bring them to fullness" (Mt 5:17). The law which He proclaims calls for total commitment without reservations.

Jesus' absolute authority as a teacher, His will to announce an inviolable "law" is extraodinarily accented by the "For I tell you" (Mt 5:20-43) repeated seven times. The number seven signified to the Jews plenitude, the expression of fullness. Thus it was immediately clear to every single listener of the Sermon on the Mount that Jesus did not intend to merely interpret the Decalogue, but rather that He proclaimed that law which characterizes the fullness of the time both in His person and in His teachings.

The evangelist, however, utilizes every literary means to dispel doubts. Here we have much more than a commentary or noncommittal pious advice. That is why we find such a powerful conclusion which appears in Matthew and Luke in almost the same words: "Therefore, everyone who listens to these words of mine and acts on them will be like a sensible man who built his house on rock. . . . But everyone who listens to these words of mine and does not act on them will be like a stupid man who built his house on sand . . ."(Mt 7:24-27). Salvation and damnation are decided by allegiance, fidelity, dedication to the Lord and the law of the New Covenant. Christ alone is the rock. But it is not enough to say, "Lord, Lord." "When the day comes many will say to me, 'Lord, Lord, did we not prophesy in your name, cast out demons in your name, work many miracles in your name?' Then I shall tell them to their faces: I have never known you; away from me, you evil men!" (Mt 7:21-23). There is no substitute for fidelity to the law of the New Covenant. The only decisive question is whether or not we keep the word of Jesus.

The law of the Covenant is not a contract between partners with equal rights. It is a gift of the Emmanuel. It is an offer of pure grace. However, a characteristic of the Covenant and its "law" is that it has been accepted freely and wholeheartedly by those who have been called. It is clearly indicated in the literary conclusion of the entire sermon. "Jesus had now finished what he wanted to say, and his teaching made a deep impression on the people because he taught them with authority, and not like their own scribes" (Mt 7:28-29). The people acclaimed the blessed revelation of God's loving design to save man. They understood the invitation: "After he had come from the mountain large crowds followed him" (Mt 8:1).

Universal Calling to Sanctity

The rallying call of all men to faith in Christ and of all Christians to holiness is the core of the Second Vatican Council's *Constitution on the Church*. The teachings of the Second Vatican Council reflect the Sermon on the Mount and the farewell speeches of Jesus in the Gospel according to St. John.

Jesus faces the crowd. The Apostles whom He had called by name and the disciples gathered around Him are in close contact with the entire people of God. His "Happy are you" and His call to sanctity apply to everybody. In praying for unity among His Apostles, Jesus intends unity and love among all His disciples so that the world may discover the faith. Even though the prayer of the Apostles precedes the prayer for all the faithful, what He is praying for is, nevertheless, the same in both cases. The Apostles represent all the faithful (Jn 17:6-26).

Jesus gives everything to everybody: Himself, the plenitude of the beatitudes. But He also demands everything from everybody: an undivided loyalty to His words. Though the emphasis on the crowd's presence at the proclamation of the morality of the beatitudes obviously leaves room for a difference in services, it nevertheless excludes the possibility of two kinds of morality—one of perfection for a small group, and another of mere minimal demands for the masses. *Both* are called upon by the same message and the same law.

Early Christian teachings make the calling to sanctity as explicit as possible, especially in demands which are most violently opposed to a legal minimalism. Thus, when the Lord speaks of self-denial as a criterion of discipleship, His words are introduced in Matthew by the words, "Then Jesus said to His disciples" (Mt 16:24). Luke introduces the same phrase with: "Then to all he said" (Lk 9:23). And so it becomes clear that "disciples" means everybody who wants to be worthy of the name Christian. Mark expresses the same truth with even greater emphasis: "And

He called to Him the multitude together with the disciples, and said to them, 'If anyone wants to be a follower of mine, let him renounce himself and take up his cross and follow me' " (Mk 8:34-35).

There is no possibility here of settling for mere mediocrity. Every Christian is addressed in the Sermon on the Mount: "You are the salt of the earth. But if salt becomes tasteless, what can make it salty again? It is good for nothing, and can only be thrown out to be trampled underfoot by man" (Mt 5:13).

The greatness of this obligation is frightening. If we understand it the wrong way, it may even lead us to discouragement and despair. The fact that Jesus did not begin with the demand but with the Good News is yet to be shown in the light of the Sermon on the Mount. One who has encountered Christ, who has received His word faithfully and entrusted himself to Him, and begins to taste the happiness of His friendship, sees nothing else in the greatness of the demand but the expression of the honorable calling, of the sincere friendship of the Lord.

Static and Dynamic Morality

The normative value of the Sermon on the Mount is beyond any doubt. Nobody may dare to remove even a dot from it (Cf Mt 5:18). However, we have to scrutinize the text very closely in order to understand what kind of normative validity is meant.

The Sermon on the Mount—through its literary form—makes it clear that we are concerned here with a kind of norm and directive which is different from all the scribes (and the Decalogue). "You have learnt how it was said to our ancestors: 'You must not!' " (Mt 5:21). There bare prohibitions are mentioned, "border norms" and limitations that are to guarantee a minimum of order and justice.

The validity of certain prohibitions is not questioned at all by the Sermon on the Mount. On the contrary the prohibitions of the Decalogue remain valid. Yet the decisive shift of emphasis should be noticed: It is not enough for a Christian merely to avoid the violations mentioned in the Ten Commandments; he has to strive unflinchingly toward the heights described by the norms of the Sermon on the Mount.

Finally, all the demands of the Sermon on the Mount point toward that height which is expressed in the words: "You must therefore be perfect just as your heavenly Father is perfect" (Mt 5:48). It means, in this context, that God's infinitely merciful love for man is the ideal after which the life of the disciples must be remodeled.

Here man is presented with a goal for his strivings which is both an honor and a goal which can never be reached completely as long as we remain in a state of pilgrimage in this life. To the question of how far such a striving obliges us we reply: "With all your heart, with all your soul . . ."(Mt 23:37-38).

The Gospel according to St. Matthew offers us a key to understanding such that we put an end to all rigorism in our relationship to our neighbors, to our despondency as well as to our indolence. In the parable of the talents the Lord praises equally the one who had added two talents to his original two and the one who had made five more with his original five talents (Mt 25:14-30). The grace of God itself becomes our teacher. "Each one of us, however, has been given his own share of grace, given as Christ allotted it" (Eph 4:7).

The "For I tell you" of the Sermon on the Mount offers

a dynamic norm which can be "fulfilled" only through constant striving in a manner roughly like that which Paul expressed for himself and every Christian: "I can assure you, my brothers, I am far from thinking that I have already won. All I can say is that I forget the past and strain ahead for what is still to come; I am racing for the finish, for the prize to which God calls us upwards to receive in Christ Jesus. We who are called 'perfect' must all think in this way" (Phil 3:13-15).

The true disciple of Christ is never self-complacent. On the other hand, he never yields to despondency. However far one might be from one's goal, if one only sets out seriously to reach with one's will for the lodestars of the Sermon on the Mount, one is already included in the "Happy are you."

CHAPTER TWO

Good News
and the Commandments

From God's point of view, the Good News of his condescending love already appears in the Old Testament as the golden background of the moral demand. The gift of the Covenant is infinitely greater than that which is imposed as a command in the Decalogue. As part of the Covenant, the Decalogue also becomes an eloquent expression of the goodness of God who wants to guide His people on the road to salvation. It is because of the hardheartedness of the many, however, that fear of punishment, the fear of God's wrath became more prominent in the Old Testament.

In the New Testament, Christ's moral message is distinctly announced as Good News. It is impossible to see it apart from the joyful message of salvation; the "For I tell you" of the moral directives receives clear-tone echoes of "Happy are you" repeated nine times. Grace precedes the commandment; faith comes before morality. In no way, however, is morality being depreciated, but its only relevant foundation is clearly indicated. "Does this mean that we are using faith to undermine morality? Not at all: we are placing morality itself on a firmer footing" (Rom 3:31).

In our attempt to clarify and to elaborate on this relationship of the Gospel message to the Decalogue, we shall first concentrate on the Holy Scripture in order to see better how the Lord, and subsequently the Infant Church, related the Good News to the moral demands. We shall then be in a position to ask ourselves: what meaning does this have for us today in regard to moral instruction and personal motivation?

Conversion through the Joyful Acceptance of the Good News

The Gospel according to St. Mark lacks the Sermon on the Mount as such; furthermore, nowhere does it offer a systematic attempt to present the moral message of Jesus in synoptic form. However, it contains possibly the oldest attempt of the Infant Church to describe the Sermon of Jesus in a very brief synthesis. Reference here is to Mark 1:14-15 which at times has also been called the *Ur-Evangelium* ("original gospel"). In this text the basic relationship between faith and morality finds expression—an expression further developed in the Sermon on the Mount.

For the impact of the message it is important to get a close look at the context. Jesus, obedient to the will of the Father, submits to the rite of the baptism of penance through John, giving an early indication that He will take upon Himself that baptism on the cross which will bring salvation to all men. For this, He has been sent and anointed by the Holy Spirit. "At the moment when he came up out of the water, he saw the heavens torn open and the Spirit, like a dove, descending upon him. And a voice spoke from heaven: 'Thou art my Son, the Beloved; on thee my favor rests'" (Mk 1:10-11). The Spirit drives Jesus out into the wilderness where He remains for forty days and nights. At this eventful introduction, the Jews probably remembered the promulgation of the law of the Old Covenant. "Yahweh said to Moses, 'Put these words in writing, for they are the terms of the covenant I am making with you and with Israel.' He stayed there with Yahweh for forty days and forty nights, eating and drinking nothing. He inscribed on the tablets the words of the Covenant—the Ten Words" (Ex 34:27-28).

In the light of this parallel we have good reason to consider the following words as synthesizing the whole preaching of Jesus and summarizing the Covenant and its law: "There he proclaimed the Good News coming from God. 'The Time of favor has come,' he said, 'and the kingdom of God is close at hand. Be renewed in your mind and believe the Good News'" (Mk 1:14-15).

No doubt, Jesus demands a total change of heart and consequently a total change in one's entire life. But the demand is preceded by the happy announcement that the time of grace has come, that God intends to guide us by the power of His merciful love and that He wants to summon us to His kingdom. The great change comes about through the belief in the Good News. Faith is the grateful and joyous acceptance of the message and the messenger, a trusting surrender of one's self to the approaching Good News and grace. He, who in his heart and soul believes this, is a new man. Christian morals rest on faith; they receive their strength from the joy of salvation.

Morality of the Beatitudes

The Pharisees who revealed themselves inimical to the Good News put on a gloomy look to let men know that they were fasting (Cf Mt 6:16). The characteristic feature of the moral message and the religion of Jesus, however, is *joy* even in the midst of the tribulations of life. The Sermon on the Mount begins nine times with "Happy are you." God's own bliss, the happiness of salvation is passed on to the disciples. Christians derive their strength for humility, for sorrow and repentance, for gentleness, for a consuming zeal for God's justice, for compassion, for pure love and even love of enemies from their joy in the friendship of God and from a gratitude overflowing with joy for Christ's convenant of love. To the extent that the disciples of Christ understand and taste the "happiness of the kingdom of God, they will bring the peace of Christ to the world and they will fulfill the great commandment of love even in the midst of contradictions, suffering, and persecutions" (Mt 5:3-12).

The reverse is equally true and important: Only by taking seriously the directives contained in the Beatitudes can the disciples of Christ preserve and augment the joy of salvation.

The moral message of the Sermon on the Mount runs counter to the petty desires of man possessed by his Ego, but at the same time it appeals to the deepest desires of his human heart for joy and happiness. Already in the law of the Covenant on Mount Sinai, the "You shall not" is a result of the Covenant, a result of the fact that God Himself, having released His people into freedom and wanting to take possession of them for Himself, thereby wants to unite them. However, the moral imperative still sounds a threatening "You shall not," because the final time of favor, the full joy of salvation, the whole strength of faith were not yet manifest. With the coming of the Incarnate Son of God, the situation changes; the moral demand of the "Happy are you" resounds with gladness. In Christ, the Father reveals His infinite love for man in such a way that the law of God is thereby written into the heart and mind of man in the form of a liberating law, bringing both peace and joy. A Christian can experience this daily if more and more he orients himself completely toward Christ and His Good News.

Christ is the true light that has come into the world in

order to illumine everything and to fill the earth with its warmth. In Him, indeed, His followers also become "light." The Good News: "You are the light of the world" implies the mission: "Your light must shine in the sight of men, so that, seeing your good works, they may give praise to your Father in heaven" (Mt 5:14-16).

This basic relationship between the Good News and the moral directive, between faith and morality, is only conceivable because the Good News is more than mere human verbiage. He who proclaims the Good News is identical with the Word of the Father. Jesus speaks with authority. His wondrous deeds are an eloquent expression for the fact that what He stands for will be achieved. The disciples are able to hear the words of Christ and act upon them (Cf Mt 7:24), because Christ's words "are both spirit and life" (Cf Jn 6:63). He will send the life-giving Spirit.

This truth is expressly revealed to our experience of faith in the Sacraments. They are effective signs and powerful words of the love of God which make us sharers of the covenant of the love of Christ with His Church. This is best expressed in the Gospel according to St. John. The speeches of Jesus about the power of faith in Him Who is the true life, the bread of life come down from heaven, are summed up in the promise of the Eucharist (Jn 6). The moral of the beatitudes centers around the Last Supper (Jn 13-14). In Jesus' farewell message, the great New Commandment is entirely an issuance of the Good News the highest pledge of which is the Eucharist. The proclamation of the commandment: "This is my commandment: love one another as I have loved you" (Jn 15:12) is accordingly introduced by the beatitude: "I have spoken thus to you so that my joy may be in you, and your joy complete" (Jn 15:11).

Beatitude and Division of the Spirits

The entire structure of the Sermon on the Mount in the Gospel according to St. Matthew makes it clear that the moral of the beatitudes is anything but a non-committal sentimentalism. Because the commandment approaches man through the Good News and the powerful deeds of God, it has divisive power as it is pointedly expressed in the Letter to the Hebrews: "The word of God is something alive and active; it cuts more keenly than any double-edged sword, piercing as far as the place where the life and spirit, joints and marrow divide; it sifts the purposes and thoughts of the heart" (Heb 4:12).

The brief treatment of the Sermon on the Mount in Luke expresses these facts from the very beginning by contrasting four beatitudes to four "Alas for you." Luke who preached and wrote for the Christians among the heathen selected four beatitudes probably in resemblance to the four cardinal virtues well-known among the Greeks. Thus his listeners could understand that the Lord had brought and announced the fullness of joy and peace. However, one who cannot bring himself to an honest commitment when faced with the fullness of salvation, when faced with the Son of God Who sacrifices Himself on our behalf, chooses the full number of the "Alas for you" also. Not only does the imitation of Christ receive subsequent external reward; more still, it carries with it honor, joy and bliss. To the same extent, disbelief and turning away from the moral demands of love automatically give birth to the "Alas for you." The sinner who remains stubborn in spite of God's infinite love is passing judgment on himself.

In Luke, the four "Blessed are you" and the four "Alas for you" are sharply contrasted to each other and are immediately followed by the commandment that divides the spirits: "But I say this to you who are listening: Love your enemies, do good to those who hate you, bless those who curse you, pray for those who treat you badly" (Lk 6:27-28). One who is completely penetrated by the truth that God wanted to choose us poor sinners to be His sons and daughters, and brothers and sisters of His only-begotten Son, has a heart filled with so much joy and gratitude that he also recognizes his enemies as brothers redeemed by Christ. However, he who wants to be haughty and harsh to his brothers in spite of God's condescension and the death of the Redeemer, delivers himself to the "But alas for you."

The "yes" of faith to the Good News and the sharing in the joy of the Lord are unthinkable without a thorough change of man's heart whereby the whole spectrum of his activities and his entire life change gradually. The extent to which the "Blessed are you" resounds bright and en-couraging, man is unrelentingly called upon to reach a decision: "There is no such thing as a good tree producing worthless fruit, nor yet a worthless tree producing good fruit. . . . A good man produces good from the store of good within himself; and an evil man from evil within produces evil. For the words that the mouth utters come from the overflowing of the heart" (Lk 6:43-45). In the longer version of St. Matthew, the passage about the tree and the fruit is directly viewed in the perspective of the criteria for discerning spirits. This discernment, however, presupposes in turn the separation of men in view of the Good News (Mt 7:15-19). The parable of the tree and its fruit appears again in St. Matthew in the invectives against the blas-phemers (Mt 12:22-37). More sharply expressed yet is the message that the humanity of Christ is destined to be a sign which men reject: many shall stand or fall because of him. "Make a tree sound and its fruit will be sound; make a tree rotten and its fruit will be rotten" (Mt 12:33).

Conclusions for Christian Wisdom and Teaching

In comparing the four classic syntheses of the Sermon of Jesus in the Gospels we are confronted with several far-reaching conclusions for doctrinal and moral instruction, and for the moral and religious life of every individual and every community.

(1) One may distinguish between doctrinal and moral teachings but one must not separate the two. A presentation of religious doctrine in a mainly polemic attitude toward those who err, and as a consequence, the dissolution of doctrinal synthesis into mere sentences for the intellect, is no better than the offering of adulterated wine. One must not sterilize the message of faith. Faith can be taught rightly as a creed only if it is done by a heart filled with the joy of faith. The message of faith is a testimony and it contains the essentially powerful motivations for the direction of one's life.

Moralism must also be avoided. In the Gospels, we do not find a "mere moral"; the commandment never appears all by itself; it is always the outcome of the Good News. Christ is both the life and the way. When morals are proclaimed in keeping with the Sermon on the Mount, when they are lived and taught in the same spirit, then that which the pious man of the Old Testament has already sensed becomes even more apparent in the life of Christians: "His words are sweeter than honey, even than honey that drips from the comb" (Ps 19:10). "Your law is what I love. Seven times daily I praise you for your righteous rulings" (Ps 119:163-164).

(2) Christian morals are not merely an abstract system. They are essentially an encounter with the Lord in the community of His disciples. Only loving persons and communities of love can communicate the morals of joy and love.

(3) In Christian life, in moral pedagogy, joy plays an all-decisive role. The function of Christian self-renunciation is above all to remove that which could obstruct the joy of faith. Sorrow in accordance with salvation presents a beatitude in itself, because repentance and conversion serve to open us widely to the joy of Christ. Joy and messianic peace are essentially inseparable. A Christian, then, will make every effort to cultivate joy and peace at every level. We rejoice in everything God has created, in the flowers of the fields, in the magnitude of the firmament, in the achievements of science, and in the beauty and dignity of the human race. More and more we open ourselves to joy through the art of making others happy. Gratitude is that art which is able to rejoice in the goodness of others and which expresses this joy in the proper spirit. The last and deepest source of all joy, however, is God Himself. That is why the Christian will take time out to meditate on God's love and the Good News. "The joy of Yahweh is our stronghold" (Ne 8:10).

B

CHAPTER THREE

The Commandment of Love

Seven times in the Sermon on the Mount the Lord begins with the phrase: "But I tell you." The number seven symbolizes "fullness." In this case it expresses the fullness of the authority of Jesus; He teaches the law of the New Covenant with authority. When He says "For I tell you" for the seventh time, His entire teachings are summed up at last. It is the commandment of perfection, the call to imitate the love of the heavenly Father: "Love your enemies and pray for those who persecute you; in this way you will be sons of your Father in heaven, for he causes his sun to rise on bad men as well as on good, and his rain to fall on honest and dishonest men alike. For if you love those who love you, what right have you in claiming any credit? Even the tax collectors do as much, do they not? And if you save your greetings for your brothers, are you doing anything exceptional? Even the pagans do as much, do they not? You must therefore be perfect just as your heavenly Father is perfect" (Mt 5:44-48). We do not truly become children of the heavenly Father until we try to make His merciful and all-encompassing love the basis of our life.

Essentially, then, the call to holiness means nothing else but the call to compassionate, sympathetic and active love of one's neighbor in accord with the ideal and the example of God. The emphasis apparently lies on compassion. St. Luke, in his shorter wording of the Sermon on the Mount, interprets the commandment, "Be perfect," very briefly with the words: "Be compassionate as your Father is compassionate" (Lk 6:36). The most important thing for a Christian is to believe wholeheartedly and to recognize by his life that God is love, and that He has created and redeemed us for the purpose of loving Him and with Him and through Him our neighbor. God reveals to us His countenance, the ways of His love; thus He reveals to us the true face of a love which represents the fullness of Christian morality.

"Show us the Father"

Our heavenly Father reveals the ways of His love to us because He really and truly wants to make us His sons. If we know Him, our conduct will reflect our identity as His sons and daughters. Philip says to Jesus: "Lord, let us see the Father and then we shall be satisfied" (Jn 14:8). Jesus replies: "To have seen me is to have seen the Father.... You must believe me when I say that I am in the Father and the Father is in me" (Jn 14:9-11). The great mission of the Incarnate Word aims at making His Father's love on earth completely known. This is emphasized by the introductory verses to chapters 13-17 of the Gospel according to St. John which are the ultimate and greatest tenets of Christian morality in the Holy Scripture. "He had always loved those who were his in the world, but now he was to show the full extent of his love" (Jn 13:1). The Father's plan of salvation is to choose us as His sons and daughters through His beloved and only-begotten Son. He loves us together with His Son and through His Son. The Son passes on the love of the Father to us. "As the Father has loved me, so I have loved you" (Jn 15:9). In His infinite love for us, Christ is the visible image of the invisible God (Cf Col 1:15; II Cor 4:4). Through Him we truly come to a knowledge of God's love for us.

Because Jesus has revealed the love of the heavenly Father unto His death on the cross, He can also restate the commandment of the Sermon on the Mount in the new law of His farewell, "Be perfect as your heavenly Father," without any change in meaning: "This is my commandment: love one another as I have loved you" (Jn 15:12). The imitation of Christ entails the imitation of the heavenly Father in His compassionate love.

The love of Jesus for us is the love of the Redeemer, i.e., a compassionate love that brings salvation. "A man can have no greater love than to lay down his life for his friends" (Jn 15:13). However, we are not the friends of Jesus by nature. Because of sin we were rather considered the enemies of God. Thus the love of Jesus until His death on the cross is love for His enemies: not only those who were instrumental in His crucifixion, but also those for whose sake He died on the cross. We can only be His friends because through infinite compassion, He has chosen us as His friends. "You did not choose me; no, I chose you" (Jn 15:16). Ultimately the love of the Redeemer reshapes us in such a way that we truly become sons of God before all men. It becomes evident that the fruit of redemption and the true result of Christian morals are that we make the heavenly Father and Christ known to all men through our love. "In the same way your light must shine in the sight of men, so that, seeing your good works, they may give praise to your Father in heaven" (Mt 5:16). Good works encompass everything that originates from a loving heart and makes known the true face of love.

In this context we understand the veneration of the saints. We look up in gratitude to the true disciples of Christ who make the imitation of Christ (and consequently the imitation of the heavenly Father) credible and concrete in ever-new historical relationships. The calling of all men

to holiness implies, above all, the command to make the
love of God intelligible to one another, helping one another
to visualize it. Gratitude for our neighbor's love for us and
our own daily striving to become for him a reflection of
God's kindness, sharpen our vision of the love of the invisible God who wants to become visible in Christ and in
all our brothers. "We ourselves saw and we testify that
the Father sent his Son as savior of the world. . . . We ourselves have known and put our faith in God's love toward
ourselves. God is love and anyone who lives in love lives
in God, and God lives in him" (I Jn 4:14-16). Because
Jesus revealed to the world the love of the Father and because He chose us for His disciples and friends, we can
say: "Even in this world we have become as He is" (I Jn
4:17). We are privileged to spread the news of God's love,
thus experiencing our greatest hope in Faith. Any conscious
lack of brotherly love, however, obscures the image of God
to our neighbor and diminishes our hope. "For how can
he who does not love his brother whom he sees, love God,
whom he does not see?" (I Jn 4:20).

This exchange of God's love is the core of spirituality
in marriage. "A man . . . is the image of God and reflects
God's glory" (I Cor 11:7). However, this he is only insofar as he fulfills his mission: "Husbands should love their
wives just as Christ loved the Church and sacrificed himself for her" (Eph 5:25). A husband who loves his wife in
accord with the love of Christ so enriches her life that she
is able to return this love. At the same time, she envisions
more fully the love of Christ and that of the heavenly
Father. The love given is returned as a stream of God's
love and draws both the lover and the beloved closer to
the love of God. "For a man to love his wife is for him to
love himself" (Eph 5:28).

With his teachings about marriage St. Paul wants to

help the wife realize Christian love within the system of the patriarchal family and thus experience in humility and inner peace the great secret of love. Nevertheless, by pointing to the revelation of the love of the heavenly Father, he also provides the husband with motivation and directives which in the course of time must reshape the patriarchal system from within. A relationship between equal partners is manifest in the decisive aspect of marriage: the mutual love of wife and husband. They are called upon to attest to each other the love of God and to make it into an increasingly more meaningful experience.

This is also the core of any other calling. It is the most noble mission of a priest to announce the love of God not only in words but also through his love as brother among brothers, as the image of the heavenly Father. In gratitude he will accept the love of the faithful entrusted to him and he will return it as a servant, not as a master. Thus priests are fathers and teachers insofar as "together with all the faithful in Christ they are disciples of the Lord" (*Decree on the Ministry and Life of Priests*, Art. 9). The celibacy of priests and members of religious orders should not mean coldness and isolation. It signifies the cordial openness of unselfish love. Both priests and religious are called upon to represent to one another in their own way what married people can be to each other: witnesses of the gracious love of God. Through their unfeigned and gentle love, they aid one another in the task of manifesting to all the faithful the calling to sainthood.

The True Face of Love

An extreme situation ethics (J. Fletcher) tries to justify everything—even adultery and false oaths, abortion and

atom bombs on open towns—with the one principle of
love. Thus "unprincipled" love appears as a sphinx, a principle without a definitive content. Should we therefore no
longer speak on love or, at least, refrain from emphasizing
the all-embracing character of love? By no means. Even
in Jesus' time much was called love that was not truly love.
However, the Lord teaches His whole doctrine in terms of
love, showing us through His personality, in His example
and through all His words—particularly through the Passion,
death and Resurrection—the true nature of redeeming and
redeemed love. The Sermon on the Mount must also be
read in this perspective: it furnishes us, above all, with the
criteria needed to make our judgments, to distinguish true
love from its counterfeits.

The final and the sharpest test of redeemed love is love
of one's enemies, the strength and firmness of love precisely
at the point where we meet resistance, misunderstanding,
rejection and contempt. The heathen, the tax collectors and
the public sinners number among those who are usually
friendly to their benefactors, friends and flatterers. The man
who wants a justified claim to the honorable title of son or
daughter of God has to prove his worth before his enemies
and those persecuting him (Mt 5:44-48). The love of one's
neighbor not only prohibits murder but also anger and
any scornful, unloving word (Mt 5:22). He who wants to
please the Father with an offering must take great pains to
remove any misunderstanding and do everything possible
to be reconciled with his brother when his brother has
something against him (Mt 5:23-24). Genuine and respectful love not only rules out adultery, it also guards against
any adulterous desire (Mt 5:27-28). Redeemed love shows
neither weakness against oneself nor against one's neighbor; moreover, it is absolutely determined to remove everything blocking love. Redeemed love proves its worth in

marital fidelity, and that implies more than avoidance of divorce. The readiness to be reconciled and to keep open every road to reconciliation even bars divorcées from re-marrying (Cf Mt 5:31-33; Mt 19:9; Mk 10:11-12; Lk 16:18; I Cor 7:10). True love creates a climate of mutual confidences in a spirit of absolute sincerity and truthfulness (Mt 5:33-37). Truly great love also reveals itself in non-violence and gentleness: in the gentle force of love.

Love is even willing to forego duly acquired rights whenever there is a possibility to win over or to convince another human being through obliging love (Mt 5:38-42). Thus it is indeed necessary to keep together all the forces of love. As a housewife in the past watched over the fire and gathered all the red-hot coals, Christian gentleness takes every opportunity to increase and to manifest love so that with patience and gentleness, it may also win those who still resist love or find it difficult to love us. Thus is the meaning of the admonition, to "heap red-hot coals on his head" (Rom 12:20). Love is consequently never sat-isfied with mere defense and self-defense. It is always active, always intent to help the other human person on the road to love. "Do not let evil conquer you, but defeat evil by doing good" (Rom 12:21).

The tests of genuine love or the instructions concerning the discernment of spirits are the core of the moral teach-ings of the New Testament. Thus the Sermon on the Mount finds its counterpart in the song of songs of love: "Love is always patient and kind; it is never jealous..."(I Cor 13:14). Together with St. Augustine one can say: "Be mindful of love and do as you please" (*Commentary to the First Letter of John*, Tract. 7, No. 8 in PL 35, 2033) —but then, one must point out the true face of love. True love carries with it the entire chorus of virtues. The apostle of the Gentiles emphasizes to the Judaists who are getting lost in the maze of their legalism: "The whole of the law is summarized in a single command: 'Love your neighbor as yourself' " (Gal 5:14-15). But at the same time he is very much concerned about making it clear to everybody that true love drives out selfishness and all its poisoned doings—all mere caricatures of love. "What the Spirit brings forth is very different: love, joy, peace, patience, kindness, goodness, trustfulness, gentleness and self-control. There is no law against things like that, of course" (Gal 5:19-23).

However, in this effort, it is crucial to recognize the true meaning of love so that we will not only possess wonderful descriptions in words, human images and ideals. We must understand that it ultimately reveals itself in the face of Christ. This is already the key to the Sermon on the Mount. It is made even clearer to us through the great synthesis which John gives in the last discourse of Jesus, who Himself teaches the true meaning of love through His personality and His example. The human words of the Incarnate Word form a wonderful unity with His incarnate countenance. Jesus teaches through the washing of feet that love is humble; in His conversation with His somewhat dense disciples He reveals the friendly love that is always patient and kind. Finally, He points to the great secret of His death: "A man can have no greater love than to lay down his life for his friends" (Jn 15:13).

Love is More Than a Commandment

Love cannot actually be commanded as one orders any other outward service. The fact, however, that God actually commands love cannot be doubted when one reads the Sermon on the Mount or the farewell of Jesus. However, we shall never realize the full dynamism and force of the commandment unless we are fully aware of the mode in

which God commands: that we are concerned here with
something infinitely greater than a bare commandment.

Love approaches us in the form of God's self-revelation.
It shines on the countenance of Christ. It spreads to us in
His joyous proclamation of the good news of love. It in-
vades our spirit and our heart in the Beatitudes as a blessed
power and force emanating from God. God's love, as it
illuminates and embraces the world through Christ, makes
us also the light of the world. Faith is the joyous and grateful acceptance of the message of this love and it is the
trusting surrender of ourselves to Love as it approaches us
in the Incarnate Son of God. Love is the great mystery of
our Faith. That is why in Faith love also becomes the great
commandment.

The Gospel according to St. John lays special stress on
the depth and height of this mystery of which the commandment is rooted. It was not we who loved first; God
loved us first. He does not only reveal His love to us ex-
ternally. He imparts it to us as a new life. "I am the vine,
you are the branches. He who abides in me, and I in him,
he bears much fruit" (Jn 15:5). Love is an entirely personal
call that becomes full reality only for the free man. But it
is, above all, an offer. The decisive factor is the most
intimate union possible with Christ, the "remaining in
Him." The more we receive and embrace Him in Faith and
the more we surrender ourselves to Him, the more we trust
in His grace and the more we look up to Him, all the more
natural and joyful will the commandment be to us. The
image of bearing fruit is central to the Bible. It shows the
unity of Faith and morals, of spirituality and morality.

The Council clearly emphasizes this point of view as
decisive for the scientific presentation of Christian morals
and, consequently, also for the proclamation of morals.
Christian moral teaching must above all present "the lofti-

ness of the calling of the faithful in Christ." Being and remaining in Christ is, therefore, the key to understanding
the calling. It means, furthermore, that the very gifts of
God urge us "to bear fruit in charity for the life of the
world" (*Decree on Priestly Formation*, Art. 16).

A practical result of this basic relationship between the
mystery and the commandment of love will be an emphasis
on humble prayer for light, strength, joy and docility to
the operations of the Holy Spirit. The Lord reminds us of
this truth in the farewell discourse, when His proclamation
of the law of love is followed by the promise of the Holy
Spirit's assistance (Jn 16:5-15). He it is who helps us to
know and to love Christ more and more, and thus to
joyously embrace the commandment of love. The less we
look on it as a bare commandment, the more we will feel
urged to fulfill it with all the strength God grants us. And
since we become increasingly aware of love's higher demands and of our own shortcomings the more we grow in
love, we will also pray more and more, putting our trust in
God's gracious help.

CHAPTER FOUR

The Sermon on the Mount and the First Table of the Decalogue

Christ came not to destroy God's revelation in the Old Testament, but to bring it to fulfillment. This fact determines our attitude toward the Ten Commandments, or Decalogue, which is the law of the Covenant for the people of Israel. On the one hand it would be wrong to look for the totality of Christian morals in the Commandments or in a mere interpretation of them; but it would be equally wrong to forget about them completely, let alone to deny their obligation. A Christian must view the Ten Commandments in the full light of the Sermon on the Mount and the other parts of the New Testament rather than look at the Sermon on the Mount in the light of the Decalogue. The Sermon on the Mount is the fuller light, compared to which the Commandments merely present a first glimpse of God's magnitude. In the full light of the Sermon on the Mount, however, the still-somewhat-hidden glamor of the Decalogue becomes more visible to us.

"I am Yahweh, your God"

Even in the Decalogue the Good News precedes the commandment: "I am Yahweh, your God, who brought you out of the land of Egypt, out of the house of slavery" (Ex 20:2; Deut 5:6). As a consequence, God is now entitled to all of Israel's love and loyalty; she must not have any gods except the true God of the Covenant (Deut 5:7). Because God has shown His love through such powerful deeds,

Israel must understand that His love is serious; God takes His people absolutely seriously, and thus the seriousness of the commandment of love. "For I, Yahweh, your God, am a jealous God" (Deut 5:9).

Essentially, the first table of the Decalogue (the first three commandments) is an unfolding and a safeguard of the one great commandment: "Listen, Israel: Yahweh our God is the one Yahweh. You shall love Yahweh your God with all your heart, with all your soul, with all your strength. Let these words I urge on you today be written on your heart. You shall repeat them to your children and say them over lying down or at your rising" (Deut 6:4-8).

The total recognition of God's love and His lordship is expressed by the very first beatitude of the Sermon on the Mount: "How happy are the poor in spirit; theirs is the kingdom of heaven" (Mt 5:3). Humility never forgets that all the good things come from God. The "pure heart" which makes possible the vision of God (Mt 5:8) is an expression of the undivided love for God. In hunger and thirst for what is right, in readiness to suffer persecution for the sake of God's name, the seriousness of grateful dedication becomes evident (Mt 5:10-12).

The Sermon on the Mount has a long section about the worship of God which also forms the content of the first table of the Decalogue. First comes purity of intent, in prayer and in all good deeds: a man who seeks his own honor and vanity in his religious exercises and in his external works is engaging in a kind of idolatry (Mt 6:1-6; 6:16-18). The Lord's Prayer, which significantly forms a part of the Sermon on the Mount in Matthew, teaches the full meaning of worship of God as it corresponds to the full revelation of the name "Father" for God in Christ Jesus (Mt 6:9-13). It particularly stressed forgiving love, through which we open ourselves to God's compassion and glorify it (Mt 6:14-15). This is in keeping with the preaching of the prophets who emphasized time and again that our offerings will please God only if we honor Him above all through compassion for our brothers.

Full recognition of the Lord and Father in heaven is also displayed by our attitude toward earthly goods. Restless concern about temporal goods, greed and avarice are incompatible with the commandment "I am Yahweh, your God," for "you cannot be the slave both of God and of money" (Mt 6:24).

"You shall not make yourself a carved image"

In order to preserve the purity of monotheism and for the sake of loyalty to the one God of the Covenant, the commandment "You shall have no gods except me" is followed by a severe prohibition against making an image of God: "You shall not make yourself a carved image or any likeness of anything in heaven or on earth beneath or in the waters under the earth; you shall not bow down to them or serve them" (Ex 20:3-5; Deut 5:7-9).

A dispute over this prohibition and whether it would also be binding in the New Covenant, shook wide parts of the Church during the seventh and eighth centuries, in the so-called iconoclasm. The iconoclasts appealed to the Decalogue, while the orthodox defenders of images referred to tradition and to the meaning that the prohibition of images had held only in the Old Testament in relation to the story of salvation.

In the pagan environment of Israel, the worship of images was the expression of a deeply rooted and dangerous tendency: Man made himself a carved image of God. In religion it was less a matter of worshiping God for His own sake and of extending love and gratitude to Him than one of making use of the cultic aspects of religion. All too often this tendency was shown in the making of idols, and the prohibition of images of God was, therefore, a pedagogical necessity under these circumstances. It signified an appeal to the conscience of the Israelites to listen humbly to God's revelation and to refrain from making an image of God for themselves as the pagans did. Thus that wise prohibition had kept the people of Israel open for the faith and for God's plan of salvation, since He wanted to make known to us the perfect image of Himself through His incarnate Son. The essence of the First Commandment, then, is a fundamental admonition to look up to Jesus Christ in everything, to listen to Him, and to endeavor to recognize Him and through Him the heavenly Father.

If, therefore, the prohibition of idols is no longer to be taken literally, we must be all the more concerned about understanding the hidden intentions, the spiritual message. The danger of making a false image of God still remains. We overcome this danger only through deep faith, through a constant endeavor to absorb Revelation in a spirit of humbleness and to understand and preserve its meaning faithfully in accordance with the Church's teachings. Since we are all called upon to lead one another and the entire world to Christ and through Christ to a deeper recognition of God's love, we must take special care to faithfully develop within ourselves the image of Christ.

For instance, we construct a false image of God if we are hardhearted and rigoristic and if, then, we even appeal to God for the sake of our own justification. A false image of God is offered by those overly conservative Catholics, be they priests or laymen, who defend their apathy, their lack of readiness to vigilance and lack of openness with an appeal to the fidelity of God. An idol is also offered, however, by those who betray the value of fidelity for the sake of mere innovation and who appeal thereby to the living God, the Lord of history.

On the other hand, we take up the cudgels for the true image of God if personally we try to reflect the compassionate, forgiving, and patient love of God in everything—and if, at the same time, we point out humbly that we are still far removed from being a perfect image of God.

The fact that the Church of the New Covenant is permitted to have religious images obliges us to see to it that religious knickknackery and a fulsomely sentimental or a distorted and bizarre art, may not disseminate a false image of God. Who knows how much trashy religious knickknackery has contributed to the spreading of unbelief! The Second Vatican Council devoted all its care to this problem in faithfulness to the spirit of the First Commandment of the Decalogue (*Constitution on the Holy Liturgy,* Art. 122-129).

The Desecrated Image of God

The countenance of Christ radiates with the beauty of God, but the hordes of sinners dared to spit upon and desecrate His face. But even the desecrated countenance of Jesus radiates wonderfully clear the image of the compassionate, mildhearted, patient, and at the same time, just God. Finally, the glory of Easter wipes away all ignominy from Christ's countenance.

The desecrated countenance of Christ is a reflection of sin, which diminishes man himself and makes him ugly. But due to the suffering of the Redeemer, repentance, humility and compassion toward one's fellow men can renew the image of God in man.

The eye of faith, which has learned to look up to Christ, will discover the hidden image of God in every fellow man, even in one who has degraded himself most horribly or who has been deeply degraded by others. One who possesses this faith will lovingly, patiently and compassionately strive to restore the image of God in his fellow man.

The true disciples of Christ will actively cooperate, according to their possibilities, in all endeavors for the protection of human dignity, for the protection of youth and the dignity of women. It is truly a disgrace that our modern welfare society has not yet managed to come up with the means to put an end to leprosy which disfigures the face and the entire body of man. Still worse, however, is the fact that so little is done to check the seduction and corruption of the weak and the exploitation of minors, for here it is not only disfiguration of the body that is at stake, but much worse, desecration of the image of God in man.

"You shall not bow down to them"

The Decalogue is rather explicit in its warnings against the idols of the heathen: "You shall not bow down to them or serve them" (Deut 5:9). The idols of our modern world are dictators like Hitler, Stalin, Mao Tse-tung and, together with them, so many who have gained power and recognition through violence and dishonesty; today's idols are the beauty queens who are measured not according to the true standards of beauty, but with eyes full of lust. Many also make idols of certain movie and TV actors and actresses who receive a hundred times more money than the most capable scientist and scholar. They are adored to the point of becoming even more famous through the press coverage of all their scandals and repeated divorces. One appeals to them when one wants to popularize divorce and similar institutions which degrade man.

Christ has unmasked the hypocritical faces of the Pharisees. He hurled a relentless "Alas for you" into the faces of the avaricious successful men. He shattered the idols of His time. His disciples must side with Him at any time and they must take an active part in the demythologization, in the smashing of false idols. But to approach the problem negatively is not enough; it is our duty to bring to credible prominence the true values, the true heroes, the true saints in such a manner that "God remains everything in everything" always and under any condition. Aside from the actual veneration of saints that always concerns itself with those true disciples of Christ who are a living testimony to Him, we must show due admiration and respect also for the true and responsible artist, the actor, the politician, the men of science and the pioneers of social justice.

CHAPTER FIVE

The Sermon on the Mount and the Second Commandment

It is a marvelous thing that God reveals His name to us. Moses spoke to God: "I am to go, then, to the sons of Israel and say to them, 'The God of your fathers has sent me to you.' But if they ask me what his name is, what am I to tell them? And God said to Moses, 'I am who I am.' 'This,' he added, 'is what you must say to the sons of Israel: I Am has sent me to you. . . . This is my name for all time; by this name I shall be invoked for all generations to come' " (Ex 3:13-15).

In His name God turns His countenance to us permitting and encouraging us to call on Him with confidence. But through His name He also tells us that He is our Lord and we are His people. Therefore, we are to invoke the name of God only with the greatest of respect and with unswerving confidence. We utter the name of God worthily only if we are willing to entrust ourselves to Him and if we consider ourselves His property.

"You shall not utter the name of Yahweh your God to misuse it"

In His name God reveals His holiness as well as His merciful desire to turn to man as a helper and friend, as a savior and lord. The name of God means salvation and life to those, and only to those, who respond to the revelation of the holiness and grace of God in the proper manner. In a very explicit way, God warns the people of the Old Testament by the Second Commandment of the Decalogue: "You shall not utter the name of Yahweh your God to misuse it, for Yahweh will not leave unpunished the man who utters his name to misuse it" (Ex 20:7; Deut 5:11). The Sermon on the Mount contains the revelation of the name of God: "Father". Consequently, it urges the Second Commandment upon us in a new way. Jesus offers us positive instructions about the "adoration of God in spirit and in truth." But He also exposes unrelentingly those lines of conduct and manifestations of character which run counter to this. The Sermon on the Mount lashes out against those abuses which then dishonored the name of God and religion. Many times these are erroneous positions against which Christianity has to fight again and again.

"Be careful not to parade your good deeds before men to attract their notice; by doing this you will lose all reward from your Father in heaven" (Mt 6:1). In a series of sentences Jesus severely takes to task those who abuse religion as a means of self-elevation. They utter the name of God, but, in fact, they seek only their self-aggrandizement in the eyes of men. They enter their names in charitable societies affiliated with the Church; they make donations to churches and to the poor, but they are only concerned with the glorification of their own name; they pray only when they can be seen by others (Mt 6:2-6).

A glance at Church history shows us the constant temptation to misuse the name of God, yes indeed, everything that belongs to the Christian religion, for the benefit of one's own selfishness. Impious men have surreptitiously obtained Church offices with money and showed pious faces in order to raise their families to riches and power. The clerical and episcopal office has often been degraded to an ambitious career. Grandiloquent titles and pompous attire have darkened the records of the priesthood. In all this, no one has openly confessed that he was only after his own glory or the satisfaction of his vanity; it was camouflaged under the name of God and the interests of religion.

It would be rather dishonest, however, if one were to concentrate only on the seamy clerical side. How often does it happen that people at festivities, at solemn First Communions, at weddings, at funerals, are concerned more with showmanship and social prestige than with glorifying the name of God. Politicians who call themselves Christians "say religion and mean opium," as it was the case during the Opium War against China. One makes use of religion instead of serving religion and the name of God in a spirit of humility. Decisions of a religious nature are reached not in view of God's all-holy name but with temporal interests in mind. The young Karl Marx learned to despise religion when his father decided to have the entire family baptized in the hope of opening up new business opportunities. Has it not been the case of many a person who "turned" Catholic or turned away from the Catholic Church when this happened to be the price for a marriage? Have not particular princes of the Church set bad example? Such an abuse of religion may have contributed to the phenomenon of modern atheism to a considerable extent.

But it is also necessary to look at the other side of the coin: How many have turned away from the Christian religion by appealing to their conscience when, in reality, the question was one of tangible interests rather than of conscience!

When we utter the name of God or when we speak of religion, we must be mindful above all of the purity of our intention to turn our heart and mind to God and our concern must be: to honor the name of God. Then will we be protected by the name of God. This truth is already announced by the prophets and later by the particularly powerful Sermon on the Mount.

"In your prayers do not babble as the pagans do"

God calls each one of us by name. We are His property. Our response should be a prayer of gratitude and a trusting supplication. Thus will we give praise to the name of the Lord. The name of God is seriously desecrated not only when it is pronounced carelessly, by cursing and actual blasphemy, but often enough by the prayers of Christians which represent an abuse of the name of God. Therefore, the Sermon on the Mount urges: "In your prayers do not babble as the pagans do, for they think that by using many words they will make themselves heard. Do not be like them" (Mt 6:7-8). The Second Vatican Council has remained faithful to the directions of the Sermon on the Mount in its concern for the dignity of the liturgy, for understandable and beautiful prayers in churches and in our homes. When we pray together, we should give honor to God while giving a mutual testimony of our faith. Nothing is more likely to endanger the faith of young people than a sloppy and dull rattling off of prayers without real involvement and without any awe of God. Nothing strengthens our faith more than the experience of the living faith and the holy awe both of which are revealed in the good prayer of the Christian community.

Again and again our prayers will tend to become babbling if we merely repeat memorized prayers. God the Father has spoken to us through His consubstantial Word, through His incarnate Son, in words full of majesty and yet wonderful simplicity. Our prayers, too, should be the spontaneous expression of our experiences, our answer to the Word of God. Faith discovers in every happening a message and an invitation, a command of God. Our prayers become our way of hearkening to this message, our supplication that God may help us to understand His gifts and His will. Our prayers are the personal "Yes," our "Here I am" in the presence of the Word and the deeds of God.

Yet we must not become discouraged and despondent when, at times, a certain absent-mindedness creeps into our prayers. God looks to our good intentions; it is enough to try one's best to pray well, sincerely and respectfully. Our words should speak of the innermost in our heart or at least provoke kind thoughts in us.

At times it may happen that we definitely will have to make an act of contrition after a prayer or service, because our "prayer" was almost nothing more than dull babbling. Fairly often, however, we will be able to reassure ourselves of an honest effort, even though our thoughts deserted us time and again. It may eventuate in our going to God in all humility confessing our inability to pray and asking: "Lord, teach me how to pray."

"Do not swear at all"

Perjury is one of the gravest sins against the name of God. "It was said to our ancestors: You must not break your oath, but must fulfill your oaths to the Lord. But I say this to you: do not swear at all. . . . All you need say is 'Yes' if you mean yes, 'No' if you mean no; anything more than this comes from the evil one" (Mt 5:33-37).

When men who are baptized in the name of Christ make solemn affirmations or promises, then they must realize that somehow the name of Christ is always at stake: for we derive our name from His name. Through absolute sincerity, honesty, and confidence we give honor to Him.

We cover our Christian name with ignominy if we are insincere and unreliable.

The negative commandment prohibiting false oaths and the positive commandment demanding faithfulness to our oaths and promises are not abolished by Jesus, but rather strongly confirmed. It is not enough to merely avoid perjury and faithlessness to a promissory oath. He who limits his ambitions to that will find himself on the brink of the abyss time and again. Since all of us call upon the one Father in heaven and since we commit ourselves to the one Jesus Christ, our Lord, we must also strive together to create an atmosphere of absolute uprightness in the Church and in society. As long as we are still in need of oaths at crucial moments, we must squarely face ourselves and ask whether we really did everything to be genuinely simple, upright and credible in all our activities.

It goes without saying that organizations that call themselves Christian must be particularly conscious of the very special obligation to use honest methods only. Otherwise, they will desecrate the name of God together with their own Christian name, and the blame will be put on them whenever this name is defamed by the enemies of the Church.

In the course of history the question arose frequently as to whether Christ, in the Sermon on the Mount, imposed on His disciples a definite prohibition that they must not swear at all. One thing is certain: that an oath must never be an everyday affair. Furthermore Christians must evidence a spirit of penance because they failed to be definitely credible without having to swear an oath. The swearing of an oath in especially solemn situations can, however, represent a veneration of the name of God that pleases Him. Thus Christ Himself answered solemnly to the high priest when the latter questioned Him: "The words are your own" answered Jesus. "Moreover, I tell you that from this time onward you will see the Son of Man seated at the right hand of the Power and coming on the clouds of heaven" (Mt 26:63-64).

Since an oath is essentially a way of revering the name of God, one must ascertain before swearing that all selfishness and any insincere thoughts are absent.

"It is not those who say to me: Lord, Lord"

The name of God is representative of the might and love of God, the countenance offered us in love, and the glory and holiness that are expressed in all His deeds. By revealing His name to us and by calling us by name He takes us seriously; but we must reciprocate. He demands that we take His love and holiness seriously, too. The Sermon on the Mount particularly emphasizes this: "It is not those who say to me, 'Lord, Lord' who will enter the kingdom of heaven, but the person who does the will of my Father in heaven. When the day comes many will say to me, 'Lord, Lord, did we not prophesy in your name, cast out demons in your name, work many miracles in your name?' Then I shall tell them to their faces: I have never known you; away from me, you evil men!" (Mt 7:21-23).

We are created by the Word of God and renewed by the Incarnate Word. Therefore, the whole man, not merely his voice is to give the grateful response of love to God's revelation of His name as Lord and Father of all. Man dishonors and desecrates the name of our Lord Jesus Christ if, by his perverted deeds, he belies his acknowledgment in words. Even the gifts of prophecy and miracles is of no avail to man if he fails to use it for the praise and glory of God's name. The knowledge of God's name obliges us to a life of humble praise and adoration.

"Hallowed be your name"

It was not without any purpose that St. Matthew has handed down to us the Lord's prayer as part of the Sermon on the Mount. It represents a climax to our Lord's teaching; it is characteristic of the "law of grace." The greatness of the command might frighten us, if we were not assured of a hearing by God when we pray to Him for things pleasing in His sight. God places His own name and honor at stake through His willingness to grant us our prayers, if we ask in the way He taught us.

The Our Father is more than a mere form of prayer. We must certainly use so beautiful a formula for common prayer since it was handed down to us in the Holy Scripture. However, above all is it a matter of remaining faithful to the basic structure, the directives which Jesus gives us in the Lord's Prayer. Luke the physician who has such a fine sense of right prayer—and who also relates the Magnificat of Mary—states the Our Father in fewer words than Matthew. However, he beautifully emphasizes the essentials of good prayer.

Our prayer life depends on God's revelation of His holy name. God the Father glorified His name through Jesus Christ, His Son. He continues to glorify it through all His kindness to men. He likewise shows His holiness through His admonitions and judgments.

The first petition of the Lord's prayer is both in Matthew (6:9) and in Luke (11:2); that petition positively summarizes the Second Commandment of the Decalogue: "May your name be held holy." We pray that God Himself may show the magnificence of His name through His benign and sanctifying deeds; for when we truly are a holy people of God, then praise is given to God's name on earth.

How can we pray in all seriousness "May your name

be held holy" unless we seriously strive to give praise to God's name on earth? At the same time, this petition is a holy promise to collaborate with the grace of God for the sake of glorifying His name.

The first petition is not just a petition among others. It rather serves to keynote all the other petitions and bestows beauty on all of them. The fatherly name of God is glorified when God's merciful reign reveals itself to us and when we let ourselves be guided by His grace: "Your kingdom come." We sanctify the name of God when we fulfill His will not merely because of fear, but rather out of love—"as it is in heaven"; trustingly we pray for our daily bread and everything else we need: when we have faith in God's compassion and at the same time show compassion for our brothers; when we avoid temptation, and if led into temptation, always rely on God's grace.

Our victory over evil, a victory possible only with the help of God's grace, signifies a prelude to the final manifestation of the victory of God over evil and the prince of evil. In all our prayers we must first be concerned for the glory of God's name; then our prayers will be sincere in every respect.

CHAPTER SIX

The Sabbath
Was Made for Man

Every Sunday anew, the events of salvation found in the Sermon on the Mount and in the farewell speeches of Jesus become grace and call for the people of God. Like the more intimate circle of the disciples and the crowds of people, we too assemble around the Lord and Master to listen to His Good News and to directives for our life. "For in the liturgy God speaks to His people and Christ is still proclaiming His gospel. And the people reply to God both by song and by prayer" (*Constitution on the Sacred Liturgy*, Art. 33).

In truth, our entire life should increasingly become an answer to the Good News. Together with the Apostles, we gather around the Eucharistic table which Christ Himself has prepared for us. There we receive the highest security of love. There the Lord teaches us the great commandment anew: "Love one another as I have loved you" (Jn 15:12). He Himself explains His commandment to us: "As the Father has loved me, so have I loved you. Remain in my love; if you keep my commandments you will remain in my love, just as I have kept my Father's commandments and remain in His love" (Jn 15:9-10).

The Christian Sunday supersedes the Sabbath of the Old Testament for here, too, Christ has brought to fulfillment the commands of Moses and the Prophets. Sunday is one of the great gifts of the Lord. It is important in our life that we understand its true meaning and that we fulfill it accordingly.

Lawfulness and Love

Already in the Old Testament, God far from enslaving His people to a law, treats the people of the Covenant as friends and sons. He explains to them that His laws are an expression of His love. The conscientiousness with which the Old Testament elaborates the law's meaning is particularly noticeable in connection with the Third Commandment, "Remember the sabbath day and keep it holy" (Ex 20:8; Deut 5:12). The theme of the Decalogue, as given in the Book of Exodus, is the blessed quietude of God—a day without either beginning or end standing above the days of creation, above earthly history. The history of man on earth, however, has a beginning and an end. (See Gen 2:2-23).

By looking upward in prayer to the Creator who does not lose Himself in His creation in any way, man finds the essence of his being and manages to preserve his freedom and that of his human brother. On the "Sabbath" the creature gives praise to his creator for all His works; he experiences himself as a member of God's family. In his belief in the eternal God, he becomes constantly aware of his hope for God's everlasting faithfulness.

The version of the Decalogue given in Deuteronomy deepens the significance even more in view of society and salvation. The law to keep the Sabbath protects the dignity and freedom of everybody, even the servants: "Remember that you were a servant in the land of Egypt, and that Yahweh your God brought you out from there with mighty hand and outstretched arm; because of this, Yahweh your God has commanded you to keep the sabbath day" (Deut 5:15).

Thus Sabbath became a day of thanksgiving to the Lord for the love that He had shown to all His sons and daughters in His creation and in all His deeds of salvation. Sabbath was an ever new call to love for one's neighbor and also for the stranger (Deut 5:14) and the socially underprivileged. It is fairly obvious then, that worship of God and keeping the Sabbath can be pleasing only if they are accompanied by social justice and love. It is equally clear, however, that nothing can keep genuine justice and love more alive than the spirit of worship and common praise of God's deeds of love.

Moreover, true love is also the decisive criterion for understanding the law. A literal and narrow-minded observance wrongs the divine lawgiver when it results in the opposite of true love for one's neighbor; this truth was emphasized by the prophets. Jesus, then, brings final clarity: He was forced to emphatic clarification by those Pharisees who were fanatics of the law but who paid little attention to the deeper meaning of brotherly love.

On a Sabbath Jesus took a walk with His disciples through a cornfield. His disciples were hungry and began to pick ears of corn and eat them. The Pharisees seized on this and used it to attack Jesus for not having taught His disciples to be faithful to the laws. Jesus proves them wrong even judging by Old Testament standards: David was right when, fleeing from Saul, he took the loaves of offering and gave them to his followers, although according to the law these loaves were for the priests alone. By the same token, the many liturgical acts which require a lot of time and attention would have to be seen as violating the obligation to rest.

Jesus wanted to make it clear—less by pointing to these facts than through a conscious act and its explanation—that the Sabbath is a gift of love to man, and that therefore an act of love does not violate it, but rather fulfills it. To those watching to see whether He would heal on the

Sabbath, waiting to accuse Him, He said: " 'Is it against the law on the Sabbath day to do good, or to do evil; to save life, or to kill?' But they said nothing. Then, grieved to find them so obstinate, he looked angrily round at them" (Mt 12:1-14; Mk 2:23; 3:6).

The true meaning of God's law can be seen only by looking lovingly upward to God and around at one's neighbor. The Sabbath law represents something absolute, namely, the combination of worship of God and love of one's neighbor. However, in commanding cultic rest on a certain day, it is not absolute, but valid only to the extent that it corresponds to the primary requirements of love of one's neighbor and well-ordered self-love under the given circumstances. "What I want is mercy, not sacrifice" (Mt 12:7). God does not accept any sacrifice that cannot be made without violating justice and love. Fanatic and slavish legalism, concerned only with the dead letter of the law, sins against God's honor because it does not take into account the fact that God made the laws for man's own good. "The Sabbath was made for man, and not man for the Sabbath" (Mt 2:27). Yet this does not allow man arbitrarily to transgress God's commandments whenever it might serve his selfishness, for by being autocratic and selfish man destroys himself.

Difference Between Absolute and Statutory Laws

The law to keep the Sabbath is a positive (statutory) divine law, that is to say, it is a God-given precept which is not necessarily obliging under all circumstances or at all times. In its specific requirement that the seventh day of the week be set aside for rest, the Old Testament law has lost its validity for the New Covenant. Sunday, the first day of the week, takes the place of the Sabbath day. And no longer is refraining from work the pivotal point, but rather the common celebration of the Eucharist, the common praise of God, the constant liberation of oneself for brotherly love by celebrating the Easter mysteries in the community.

In recent times, the Lord's statement that "the Sabbath was made for man, not man for the Sabbath" has been stretched in an entirely new way by some advocates of so-called "situation ethics." In their interpretation, it is transformed into the principle "the moral law was made for man, not man for the moral law," and this principle is held to be applicable to all the Commandments. Thus, they say, no Commandment binds unconditionally except the general principle of love for one's neighbor. In borderline cases, they say one could possibly forgo any one of God's commandments without sinning, so long as he acts from genuine love.

This opinion is wrong. It is based on an erroneous understanding not only of the moral law, but also of man. There are moral laws—as for instance, the laws against blasphemy, adultery, fornication, rape and perjury—which apply always, because they are made for man and express man's nature; in transgressing such laws man would always sin against his own dignity and calling. Those laws are above all made for man, but in such a way that they appear necessarily in keeping with the nature and destiny of man as soon as man rightly recognizes himself.

The formal Commandment of love is not alone in being absolute: all the other virtues—justice, loyalty, truthfulness humility, and chastity—are definitely binding because they flow from our obligation to love God and neighbor; ultimately, they are nothing else but the true face of love. Love is not a sphinx, appearing as justice on the one side and injustice, fornication and self-mutilation on the other. We will have to return to this truth in our discussion of the second table of the Decalogue. There we have Commandments written in man's heart, which he cannot violate without sinning against God and man.

The Meaning of the Christian Sunday

Our first encounter with the Christian Sunday does not have anything to do with a bare Commandment. First of all, we must see the fact that Christ, Our Lord and Redeemer, rose on the first day of the week, bringing the powerful message of the messianic peace (Mt 28:1-7; Mk 16:1-8; Lk 24:1-8; Jn 20:1-9). Sunday is the "day of the Lord"; it is on a Sunday that the Holy Spirit descended on the Apostles. In spontaneous joy and gratitude the early Christian community gathered, preferably on the first day of the week, to celebrate the Paschal mystery in the Eucharist. Love, as the most essential law, urges the Church to give full meaning to Sunday. Concern for brotherly love, which is mainly nourished by the power of the Eucharist and the common listening to the Word of God, causes the Church to summon all her sons and daughters at least once a week, preferably on the day of the Lord. It is an invitation to joy, to growth in faith, hope and love. The celebration of the Eucharist on Sunday is an immeasurable gift of the Redeemer's love. Only apathy and shallowness could consider it as a burden or an annoying Commandment.

In celebrating the Eucharist on Sunday we look back with the joy of faith to the historical events of the Death and Resurrection of the Lord and the descent of the Holy Spirit. By virtue of our Baptism, however, the Lord's Resurrection is not only the greatest event of the past, but also the outstanding fact of salvation which has entered into our own existence. In our Baptism we have been cleansed of sin in order to live with Christ. We have received the first installment of eternal glory. Thus, the celebration of Mass on Sunday symbolizes a happy looking ahead of the Christian community, a common expectation of the second advent of the Lord who will bring everything to fulfillment. Then the eighth day without either evening or morning will set, the eternal celebration of divine love.

It is pedagogically important to refrain from speaking to children first about Sunday obligation. Before the mention of obligation, both parents and the priest should explain to the child the honor and happiness connected with the invitation to share in the Eucharist. Then, he should be helped to follow the celebration according to his age and understanding. Much will depend on the way that the entire community sings, prays and listens together with the priest to the Word of God.

But as soon as a young boy or girl really begins to grasp the values of the celebration of the Eucharist on Sunday, as soon as he or she has experienced the right manner of celebration, then will he also understand what is meant by a Commandment and why and how it obliges.

The decisive question of conscience is whether we strive to better understand the meaning of the Sunday celebration of the Paschal mystery, whether we join actively in the celebration. The question of rest on Sunday is only secondary; thus, it is above all a matter of making enough time available for prayer and meditation and not losing ourselves in worldly thoughts and activities. We must not become the slaves of either work or greed.

Borderline Cases Concerning Sunday Obligation

Finally, there remain a few border questions: Are we obligated to attend Mass on Sunday even under very special circumstances? May we take care of this or that on Sunday? However, these two questions are not on the same level. Participation in Mass on Sunday is infinitely more important than the prohibition of work on Sunday. For ages, the Church has forbidden any pettiness and scrupulosity in this respect. Where love of one's neighbor and rightly understood self-love require us to work, we may do so safely. But we must not let greed or an unbridled desire to work drive us to make a working day out of Sunday.

An urgent obligation of love excuses a person even from the obligation to attend Mass on Sunday. One might think of a mother who must attend to her sick child. By doing her duty there she is united with the celebration of the Redeemer's love. One may doubt, at times, whether the reasons for an excuse are sufficiently serious: a good criterion for judging the case is one's willingness to attend Mass during the week, if possible.

CHAPTER SEVEN

Sacraments
and the Formation of Life

Religions of all times and civilizations, including our present one, have always tended to separate liturgy from the realities of life. This, on the one hand, often led to empty ritualism with neither relation to life nor strength to transform morals and morality. Thus, scrupulous observance of ritual obligations may be found side by side with either a fixed set of morals accompanied by an irreligious narrow-mindedness and leaves no room for genuine affection; or, at the other extreme, an unbridled formlessness and corruption of morals. Barriers, often nearly insurmountable, are erected between the "sacred"—the "religious" values embodied in the ceremonials or, at least slavishly connected with the practically ceremonial—and the "profane" which constitutes the entire stream of life.

On the other hand, we frequently find a false encounter between religion and morality, in which religion simply sanctions the given morals—dubious and imperfect though they be—without really inspiring and transforming them in the spirit of worship of God.

Christ put an end to both the separation and the false encounter of religion and morality. This does not mean that Christianity would not face the same temptations again at a later time. But Christ teaches us, through example and word, that worship, genuine love for God, is to bear fruit in active brotherly love.

Because religion and priesthood are so closely related, the essence of Christ's priesthood is also the orientation for the reciprocal relationship between religion and morals, between "sacrament" and the formation of life. Christ, the eternal high priest, is not of the priestly family of Aaron, not of the tribe of Levi; He is not a priestly official. His priesthood is entirely a "worship in spirit and in truth" (Jn 4:24), and He attends to His priestly calling at the tree of the cross, in His dedication to His brothers in the manifestation of His love and in the proclamation of the Good News. Worship, the loving acceptance of the will of the heavenly Father, and the all-embracing love for man are perfectly united in His life and death. We may say that Christ predicted that the "priesthood" of officials and ritualists would be judged most severely. Although He appointed priests, it was chiefly for the purpose of witnesses to faith and love and to serve their brothers the joyous news. He does not want officials, but rather apostles who spread the Good News by word and deed and who, through their humble service, urge the "priestly people of God" to glorify Him in solidarity and through brotherly love.

Noted Biblical scholars, such as J. Jeremias, believe that Jesus' moral message as summarized in the Sermon on the Mount was "rooted in life" as an instruction following Baptism, an instruction in which the infant Church emphasized the greatness of grace and man's calling to the Church as well as the expected fruits of conversion. Already in Christ's farewell address (Gospel of St. John) we find that during the Last Supper He combined moral exhortations with the institution of the Eucharist. There, mindful of His death and Resurrection, He made known the great commandment: "Love one another as I have loved you"; at the same time He promises the descent of the Holy Spirit who will give His disciples full light and strength.

The sacraments proclaim the Good News and imply the

reciprocity of gifts. At every celebration of the Holy Eucharist, we proclaim the death of the Lord as the salvific event in an ever renewed gift and challenge. The message of our Lord's coming to us through faith: "I have died for you; I live for you and in you" likewise includes the command "Love one another as I have loved you."

The Mass is "valid" even when the priest purposely turns his back to his brothers and mutters unintelligible words, while those present around the altar pursue their own private devotion. In such a Mass, hardly worthy of being called a celebration of the Eucharist, the proclamation of the Sermon on the Mount and the farewell speeches of our Lord are expressed very imperfectly, if at all; indeed, such a Mass obscures the Good News for many people.

The Mass is "valid" even if both celebrant and community seek only the comfort of their own devotion, even if they do not open themselves to the command, "Love one another as I have loved you." However, what is the use of such a "validity," after all, when it is not what Christ meant it to be? The celebration of the Eucharist is meant to be a gift appealing to both the mind and the heart, a gift of the Redeemer's love calling for reciprocity of love, goodness, compassion and unity. The grace of the sacrament becomes an actual event of salvation only if the Good News and grace received prompt us to genuine love of neighbor.

The sacraments are visible, meaningful signs of the gift and the implications of the Christian calling. Both priests and laity shall cooperate so that all realize the full fruits of the sacraments.

A father whose eighth child had just been born came to see the old parish priest who had baptized all his other children. This time, however, he was not satisfied with merely making an appointment for the baptismal ceremony.

"Father," he said, "several times you have preached so
beautifully about the infinite value of each child and about
the gift of faith that both family and community mediate
to the children. Couldn't all that be emphasized a little
bit more during the baptismal ceremony? This time my
whole family, including the mother of the child, will be
present at the Baptism. After all Baptism is such a great
event in our and the child's life. Many friends and relatives
are invited. How about inviting the whole parish? Couldn't
the baptismal ceremony occasionally take place as a well-
attended evening devotion on Sunday? Does it not imply
honor, joy and responsibility for the entire Church when
God entrusts to her a child reborn in Baptism? After all,
the teaching about the marvelous things promised to the
child during Baptism does not merely concern the immediate family. Would it not be a good idea, then, for all
the faithful to take an active part in the baptismal ceremony
at least a few times a year, in order to renew their own
baptismal vows and thereby guarantee the newly born
child of God an atmosphere of faith, hope and love in the
Christian community?" With eyes filled with tears the parish
priest said, "Amen! That's the way we are going to do it.
All the bells shall call the faithful to the Baptism. Likewise,
our joy shall find expression in communal singing."

At the Last Supper, when Christ instituted the Holy
Eucharist, He gave His disciples the new commandment
of charity. They were all gathered close around Him and
had truly become one family through His love. The Lord
taught His disciples through the visible proof of His humble
love. Christ's humble love and service are repeated although
in various form during the celebration of the sacraments.
"Liturgical services are not private functions, but are cele-
brations of the Church, which is the 'sacrament of unity' "
(*Constitution on the Sacred Liturgy*, Art. 26).

Baptism and Confirmation establish the mystical body of Christ. In their special grace and symbolic character, they are a call to the baptized and confirmed to use all their natural abilities and supernatural gifts of grace bestowed on them in the service of love. The Eucharist is the "bond of charity" (Art. 47). To open oneself up to the grace of the Eucharist implies an essentially renewed and grateful acceptance of the community and particularly the commandment of love. In the sacrament of Penance, God's benign compassion conveys to us the most urgent command to truly love one another in forbearing and compassionate charity. In the sacrament of Matrimony Christ meets the Christian spouses to embrace them in His bond of love and faithfulness. "He abides with them thereafter so that, just as He loved the Church and handed Himself over on her behalf, the spouses may love each other with perpetual fidelity through mutual self-bestowal. Authentic married love is caught up into divine love" (*Constitution on the Church in the Modern World*, Art. 48).

From Holy Scripture, tradition and the liturgical forms, it becomes evident that the sacraments are at the same time worship of God and expressions of and call to brotherly love. In the sacraments, God glorifies Himself through His love for man, invites and urges us to glorify Him through our joint assent. We glorify the death of Christ when, with the help of God's grace, we are determined to remove everything from our aspirations and our life which could bar or falsify love.

The sacraments teach us a real lesson about man's powerlessness for loving his neighbor in a redeeming way without God's gracious help. Yet at the same time, they also tell us that there is no salvation unless we bear fruit in love for the benefit of our fellow men and to the praise of God. A mere Sunday Christian who barely meets the minimal demands of the law would be stirred from his complacency by a clear understanding of the true worship of God. In like manner, the activist, too busy to listen to the Word of God, should be awakened and recognize that his life is fruitless unless Christ shines upon him.

Signs of Faith and Hope

The sacraments are signs of faith. They are expressions of God's fidelity and truthfulness as well as the Church's faith in response to God's invitation and call. In the liturgy we gratefully receive the Word of God and joyfully surrender ourselves to Him.

The deeper the roots of faith, the more joyfully the Christian will celebrate the sacraments of faith. He who remains indifferent to the celebration of the liturgy deprives himself of the strength emanating from the community of believers. The more the individual Christian, through his joyful participation, contributes to the worthy celebration of the sacraments, the greater will be the strength derived from it.

In the sacraments Christ gives His Church the assurance of His fidelity. The response of the Christian is that of hope and confidence which proves itself genuine only to the extent of man's serious effort to reciprocate God's fidelity.

As symbols of unity, the sacraments give us the message of a hope which leads to salvation in the blessed communion of love through perfect solidarity. "Do all you can to preserve the unity of Spirit by the peace that binds you together. There is *one Body, one Spirit,* just as you were all called into *one* and the same hope when you were called" (Eph 4:2-4).

The sacraments, when rightly understood and celebrated, help us to break the fetters of our self-centeredness leading us towards a genuine, selfless concern for our neighbor's salvation.

Karl Marx believed that religion would, by necessity, alienate man from his earthly task. Not only would the pious man lose precious hours with useless religious activities, but worse yet, he would also lose his sincere interest in the social order. Yet, in reality, true piety is a powerful motive for one to capitalize on the present opportunities in the shaping of a Christian social order. It is the hope and expectation of the "new heaven and the new earth" which during the celebration of the Sacred Liturgy challenges us to greater vigilance for the kairos, the opportunities of the present moment. Christian hope not only delivers us from wrong attachments to transitory things, but likewise, teaches us the value of created things as gifts from God entrusted to man for true and concrete expressions of brotherly love.

All the sacraments transmit the message of God's compassionate love as foundations of man's hope. In Baptism, we are liberated from sin. God's long-suffering patience is glorified in the sacrament of Penance. The all-holy God in His compassionate forgiveness of our sins expects a similar attitude in our hearts. How would we pray with confidence: "Forgive us our trespasses" if we make no efforts to be compassionate ourselves as the Father in Heaven: "as we forgive those who trespass against us" (Lk 6:36; Mt 6:12). "Yes, if you forgive others their failings, your heavenly father will forgive you yours; but if you do not forgive others, your father will not forgive your failings either" (Mt 6:14).

If the Good News of God's compassionate love as revealed through Jesus Christ does not totally change our lives, then our hopes will be in vain. The Sermon on the Mount is very specific on this point and completely in line

with the preachings of the Prophets who, in dealing with
the ritualists again and again emphasized compassion as
the only sacrifice pleasing to God. "Do not judge, and you
will not be judged; because the judgments you give are
the judgments you will get, and the amount you measure
out is the amount you will be given. Why do you observe
the splinter in your brother's eye and never notice the
plank in your own?" (Mt 7:1-3). Our brothers' worst
offenses are no more than splinters in comparison with our
offenses against the merciful and all-Holy God. How could
hardhearted man, unwilling to release his brother from
the debt of a few pennies hope for compassion from the
heavenly Father? It was God who first revealed His grace
to us. In turn, His merciful kindness becomes for us the law
of holiness so that we too may show mercy and compassionate love.

Each sign of divine compassion strengthens our hope
for eternal life, but only to the degree that we are willing
to learn from it. Veneration of Mary as the mother of mercy
redounds to the greater glory and praise of God if her example impels us to compassion for our brother who is in
need. Hardheartedness to our brothers indicates that our
veneration of Mary is mere sentimentalism.

Christianity as a whole is a witness to God's grace.
Accepted by God's merciful love each Christian received the
urgent mission of witnessing to God's goodness and compassionate love—not so much by marches and public
demonstrations of faith but rather by an all-embracing,
non-discriminating charity for the needy. The song "Praise
to the Lord for His Compassion Lasts Forever" only has
meaning if it sharpens our ear for God's word: "I have
given you an example so that you may copy what I have
done to you. . . . Now that you know this, happiness will
be yours if you behave accordingly" (Jn 13:15-17).

Worship of God in Spirit and in Truth

Jews and Samaritans were quarreling regarding the place of proper worship of God. Jesus' answer is: "But the hour will come—in fact it is here already—when true worshippers will honor the Father in spirit and in truth: that is the kind of worshipper the Father wants. God is spirit, and those who worship must worship in spirit and in truth" (Jn 4:23-24). Jesus Himself is so anointed with the fullness of the Spirit that He sacrifices Himself for his brethren in order to give praise to the infinite love of God. Jesus not only proclaims through words and signs that God is love; He worships the heavenly Father "in truth" by loving His friends in this world to the very last.

Liturgical, private and communal prayers are all intended to lead us to that kind of worship in which we address God "in spirit and in truth." Even if we say the "Our Father" in the privacy of our room, we are still united in the common bond of God's fatherhood. The Holy Eucharist as well as the other sacraments bring this same message home to us. Together with Christ who "did not think of Himself" (Rom 15:3) we are united before God as one family.

The love and example of our Lord and Redeemer by which He glorified the heavenly Father invites us through Scripture, liturgy and the word of God "to be tolerant with each other, following the example of Christ Jesus, so that united in mind and voice (we) may give glory to the God and Father of our Lord Jesus Christ" (Rom 15:5-6).

These sentiments of unity should be expressed in the manner in which we celebrate the sacraments so that our whole life may be shaped by it and become a witness. "Through him, let us offer God an unending sacrifice of praise, a verbal sacrifice that is offered every time we acknowledge his name. Keep doing good works and sharing your resources, for these are sacrifices that please God" (Heb 13:15-16).

Active, loving concern for the temporal well-being and the eternal salvation of our fellow men is the most fitting expression of true worship of God.

CHAPTER EIGHT

Love of Neighbor and Expression of Neighborly Love

The greatest concern for a Christian is "to remain in the love of Jesus," just as Jesus Christ remained in the love of the Father (Jn 15:10). Jesus reveals to the world the full extent of His Father's love and of His own love for the Father through His mission to embrace all men in His redemptive love. Thus it is that the love of God also teaches Christ's disciples the other great commandment: "Love one another as I have loved you" (Jn 15:12). Adherence to this one commandment designates the discipleship of those remaining in Jesus and with Him in the heavenly Father. "His commandments are these: that we believe in the name of his Son Jesus Christ and that we love one another as he told us to" (1 Jn 3:23).

It will now be shown how love of neighbor is manifested in the Beatitudes, in the works of mercy, in the virtues, and finally, in the commandments of the second table of the Decalogue.

Sentiment and Act

"Happy the pure in heart: they shall see God (Mt 5:8). If man in his innermost being is pure, if his intentions are truly aimed at his fellowman, then the love of neighbor will bring happiness to both the lover and the beloved, and this love will be blessedly transformed into an ever better understanding of the love of God. Love is the dedication to the "you" in a spirit of respect and reverence, distance and closeness. The true sentiment of love accepts the other human being as a person, discovering the image of God even behind a mutilated face. Love seeks community, but a community of individuals who act according to their own conscience and reasoning, a community without exploitation and equalitarian pressures. Love is benevolence but not of the condescending kind; love wants the best for the other human being because it believes in the great potentialities of the other man. Love is pregnant with hope for one's fellowman because it is aware of the all-embracing love of God. If one honestly wishes the best for his fellowman, then he will also want to serve him whenever he stands in need and whenever God affords us the opportunity to succor him.

Humility is the surest path to love. "Happy are the poor in spirit" (Mt 5:3). Whoever appears poor before God receiving everything from His hand gratefully and humbly will also be accepting the love of his neighbor. And this is one of the most precious characteristics of Christian love. He who is only impressed with how much good he has done, does or should do to others, elevates himself and in so doing, he looks down on the other man. Only the person who accepts the love of others in a spirit of simplicity will succeed in giving love without humiliating others.

Love delights in truth (1 Cor 13:6) and mourns together with those in sorrow. "How blest are those who mourn; they shall find consolation" (Mt 5:4). He who, with the help of God's grace, weeps with the sorrowful in undivided solidarity also succeeds in mourning his own sins, his offences against God, in a redemptive way. On the contrary, he who cannot be moved by the physical, psychological and spiritual needs of his fellowman will only continue his conversation with the serpent, even in his contrition before God, entangled as he is with his egocentricity. Genuine compassion first finds expression in helpful words and ways. Already in his earthly life such a man will harvest plentiful blessings; he will comfort others and not invert to his own petty Ego.

"How blest are those of a gentle spirit; they shall have the earth for their possession" (Mt 5:5). Gentleness is the smouldering energy of love. The angry and impatient human being wastes away the energy of his being in a fruitless manner. To be sure, love can also get angry for the very reason that it takes the other human being seriously and because it wants to remove everything that could be a deterrent to the welfare and salvation of others, the community, or their rightly understood interests. Anger from true love is entirely different from the anger of the selfish and proud man. True anger is contained; it enlists the energy of love against evil in such a way that the other human being feels assured and understood in his own fight against evil. "Love is always patient and kind ... it does not take offence, and is not resentful" (1 Cor 13:4-5). The disciple of Christ knows that it is not right for him to pass final judgment on his neighbor. Precisely because in obedience to the Sermon on the Mount (Mt 7:1) he never acts like the judge of his brother, he likewise detects the need that cries out for help, even when this cry for help sounds like an accusation or an unkind word.

This attitude of gentleness, patience, and kindness not only applies to the relationship between persons but also to groups and communities. Thus, for instance, the renewal of the Church today will be a function of the concentrated and controlled love and energy on the part of the advocates of renewal. Faced with a group of boisterous representatives of an intransigent apathy who proclaim that a hundred years will not suffice to correct the mistakes of Pope John and the Second Vatican Council, it is our duty to remain firm in our hearts, determined to look ahead together with the Lord of history instead of looking for Him in the grave. Contamination by surging ill-feelings can only be avoided by mustering all of one's energies of love and understanding to counteract them. "Resist evil and conquer it with good" (Rom 12:21).

"Happy are the peacemakers; they shall be called sons of God" (Mt 5:9). Love does not approve of foul peace. It does not concede that white is black and black is white. Just as Christ evoked the contradiction of the world, especially of the hardhearted lawyers, so also the true disciples of Christ have to fight the traditionalists and impatient innovators at all times. But neither have they sided with the stubborn traditionalists against the revolutionaries nor have they fought the cause of the revolutionaries against the traditionalists. Even though the total life with Christ gives rise to defamation, scorn and persecution, the peaceableness of the disciples of Christ who are faced with defamation is a sign of the messianic peace and the effective invitation to a change of mind. The last cry of the martyr, St. Stephen, "Lord, do not hold this sin against them" (Acts 7:60) was apt to convince those Jewish-Christians, who were skeptical about his progressive thinking and even somewhat hostile, that it was here that the love of Christ was victorious. This love clearly exposed the hardheartedness of the stoners. It also left a sting in the heart of the persecutor Saul, a sting that was due to overcome him.

"Happy are those who show mercy; mercy shall be shown to them" (Mt 5:7). He who truly believes in the miracle of redemption will take every opportunity to praise God for His mercy. Yet, the best praise is doing unto our brother as He, the Father of all mercy—through His beloved Son, has done unto us. Unfeigned, unlimited forgiveness and a compassion ready to act and sympathize with those who suffer become demands of the new justice for the redeemed, for God has justified us from pure mercy since we were, indeed, sinners. Grateful love for God liberates us from the petty, bitter concerns about our own justification and lets us hunger and thirst for that justice which God has revealed through us. This grateful love makes us also mindful of the dignity and rights of our fellowman.

The Acts of Mercy

As redeemed men, we cannot ignore the question of salvation for those to whom Christ, the only Redeemer, has not yet been announced and witnessed to credibly. The question becomes frightening when one remembers what the Council said with respect to the phenomenon of unbelief in our modern world: "Taken as a whole, atheism is not a spontaneous development, but stems from a variety of causes, including a critical reaction against religious beliefs, and in some places against the Christian religion in particular. Hence believers can have more than a little to do with the birth of atheism. To the extent that they neglect their own training in the faith, or teach erroneous doctrines, or are deficient in their religious, moral, or social life, they must be said to conceal rather than reveal the authentic face of God and religion" (*Pastoral Constitution on the Church in the Modern World*, Art. 19). A thorough examination of conscience is, therefore, an absolute necessity for the charity of those redeemed in Christ. Every individual Christian, everyone, must humbly figure out how he can reveal the love of God to everybody and thus point the way to the true faith.

Christ is the original sacrament in which the Father has

perfectly revealed His love. The Church, the community of the true disciples of Christ, continues this mission by making the faith knowable through love. Therefore, in a deeper sense, we can say that those who show mercy to their suffering followmen and, above all, to their enemies, together with Christ become a sacramental sign which, by virtue of the power of the Holy Spirit, brings salvation to the world. Likewise, we can say that the poor, the despised, the embittered whose misery is crying out to us for help become either a sign of salvation or a cause of our downfall. Just as the thoughts of men, when confronted by Christ, bear witness to their fall or resurrection, so too, the physical and psychological sufferings of our neighbor become signs of salvation which must enter man's considerations in this life; through these signs man's eternal salvation is decided.

In this sense, then, the description of the Last Judgment (Mt 25) hints at the answer to our question concerning how they can be saved who do not yet know Christ. Wherever genuine love approaches them, it is a gracious gift of God arousing in them the blessed possibility of gratitude and mercy toward others. By doing good according to their possibilities and under the operations of the Holy Spirit, they find Christ without realizing it. If, however, all of us who know Christ through faith did good in accordance with the fullness of the grace of God, then we would hardly encounter the phenomenon of the "anonymous Christians" who, indeed, draw nearer to Christ through their innermost sentiments without actually knowing Him. The fact that there are men outside the Church who surpass us in their merciful love is a powerful call to do penance. Only if we hearken humbly can we fulfill our mission to attest credibly to men that we believe in Christ in whom the Father has revealed the fullness of His love.

The Christian and the Meaning of Virtue

To the Stoic who forever wants to sneak into our hearts in the guise of a Christian, virtue means above all self-pre-servation and self-perfection, if not self-aggrandizement. The emphasis on the ego bears reference to others only insofar as they have something to do with the exaltation and pro-motion of one's ego. Subsequently, the Stoic arrives at the following ethical principle: not to succumb to passions any more than is good for self-preservation, and among the passions, the Stoic lists love and compassion.

A Christian patterns his concept of virtue after the example of Christ, the Good Samaritan: he sees his brother who is in need of help, he is moved by compassion, he dresses his wounds, lifts him onto his mount and pays off his hospital expenses. He does not calculate the extent to which his own virtue has been enriched. Virtue arrives on the back of deeds performed with the "you" in mind. The mystery of Easter proclaims this at all times: He who loses himself gains everything, and finds his true self; he who seeks himself in a selfish way—even though he might be performing good deeds—loses and corrupts his true self.

Christian virtue lies in that ability to love which comes through the love of God; it is the ability to really look to our fellowman, to be grateful to him, to listen to his call, to walk up to him and honor him by doing him good. Christian virtue opens our eyes to God and our neighbor. This is precisely what is meant by conversion: to desert our egocentricity and to turn to the better opportunities for our individuality in the service of our neighbor, self-preservation through self-denial, peace of mind through the passionate dedication to the kingdom of the all-uniting love of God.

Christian virtue manifests itself in the *search for truth*:

it wants to know God and one's fellowman better and better, and with this increasing knowledge of God and one's fellowman, to know oneself better in order to love ever more truthfully. Love is truthful for, without the genuineness and truthfulness of the word, the bridge between the "you" and the "I" has no chance of holding up and it becomes undependable.

Love cannot simply be equated with *justice* for love is above all a harmony of hearts, the personal relationship between "I," "you" and "we." Justice has reference to objective things and rights; it is meant to regulate the parity of give-and-take, the external order of the community and its structures. Zeal for these orders, for laws and rights is, however, genuine virtue only insofar as persons and a decent community of persons are concerned who are called to love and to help one another become more and more capable and worthy of love. Whoever has only a slight notion of the great importance of a just order of political and economic life for peace and man's capacity for love, cannot honestly claim that he loves his fellowman if he fails to make every effort to achieve justice in private, social and political life. However, he who only clings to the letter of the law and who is only out for services according to the principle of parity without being mindful of interpersonal love, discredits justice, too; he is not truly just in the Christian sense, that is, he is unable to articulate love and he does not contribute to the love of man.

Love is the principal prerequisite for the virtue of *prudence;* prudence, however, is the eye of love, the concern about the genuine possibilities of dialogue and service, of the encounter between the "I," the "you," and the "we." Prudence is the fine tact of conscience in a concrete situation. He who loves and wants to grow in his love will attempt his best not only to acquire an abstract knowledge of the moral principles, but also a loving knowledge of human nature and conditions of life; he will also endeavor to learn from the experience and wisdom of others. Like love, the Christian virtue of prudence is always in need of growth; that is to say, we are not prudent unless we are ready to learn even from our mistakes and those of our fellowmen. We are on the right road to prudence if we are willing to humbly admit our own imprudence.

Christian love is strong-minded and valiant; it resists unswervingly the temptation of evil, no matter whether it arises from the unexpurgated abyss of a man's own being or whether it approaches us from the world around us. The Christian virtue of *fortitude* is that enduring power of love which does not give in to evil, but which itself overcomes evil in its non-violate and infinitely powerful attitude of love. The greatest act of bravery is patience and endurance when it is necessary to suffer, so that the kingdom of love might prevail over evil, and gentleness over those who make it difficult for us to love. This gentleness and persevering patience is only possible if, in situations of conflict, we are as concerned about the well-being and salvation of those who put us to the test as about self-preservation—preservation of community out of an unshakable love.

Christian love is manifested in the virtue of *gentleness*. Confucius ranks it among the four cardinal virtues, or as he says, "among the four most precious gifts which heaven bestows on man." It includes also the constant endeavor to learn from the good habits and manners of others; it is vigilant in its expression. Its actual source and strength is, however, loving kindness, a heart at peace in its unwavering love.

Christian love cannot sing its song if *self-control*, the combined virtues of discipline and temperance, is missing in its chorus. This virtue, however, is possible only for the sons and daughters of Adam if they deny themselves, *i.e.*, if they suppress vigilantly a false kind of self-love which would disperse and squander their energies.

Love Fulfills the Commandments

The meaning of the commandments, and above all, of those found in the second table of the Decalogue, is the protection of love. A love which is yet incomplete needs the protection and the warning signals of the commandments. The perfect love in heaven will have no more need for them. Yet it is only a growing love that gradually comes to understand the true meaning of the commandments. They are not an adjunct of love, but stand completely in the service of the love by which and in which man truly finds himself.

The *first three commandments* protect the love of God; the object of the second table is the ordering of love of neighbor, the order of love among men.

The *fourth commandment* stakes out the realm of the family, the most decisive community of love. In the respectful love for their parents, children honor the love of their parents for each other, which is the fountain of life and an especially powerful source for a good training of mind and body; ultimately they gratefully honor God for the gift of life which has been bestowed on them out of love and with respect to the fulfillment of love.

The *fifth commandment* covers the goods of physical life and the health of the whole person entrusted to men in mutual responsibility. He who is willing to spend his energies and to sacrifice his life together with Christ slowly or suddenly in the service of neighbor and community, will never sin against the health and life of his neighbor. He who lacks love erodes his own life and brings the poisoned drop of bitterness and discord into the life of many others.

Human sexuality reveals its final meaning only in faithfully dedicated love. The *sixth commandment* protects the meaning of this love in which the marriage partners not only assist each other in lovingly perfecting themselves, but, at the same time, safeguard the future of the human race. In this perspective, youth keep themselves open to the calling either to marriage or to celibacy.

The *seventh commandment* reminds us that all temporal things, even our personal capabilities are all gifts of the one heavenly Father with respect to love among his children. Only he who strives to receive everything gratefully as a gift of the love of God and who uses it as a means to express love in the community can truly be just and delight in everything.

The *eighth commandment* protects the love due our neighbor in truth and truth in love. Honesty is to be expressed in our words and deeds if, as Christians, we are to witness to the truth of salvation.

The *ninth and tenth commandments* remind us that it is impossible to maintain an external order if our hearts and our sentiments are in a state of disorder. They convey the fundamental moral appeal: "Be renewed in your mind."

The Decalogue does not comprise the entire law for a Christian; indeed, he who refuses to do anything beyond the letter of the Decalogue is far from being a true Christian. He also misunderstands the Decalogue, for, according to the intentions of God, it was to serve as a signpost leading us to the Sermon on the Mount, to the law of the New Covenant. Only he whose attention focuses on the growth of love in accordance with the Sermon on the Mount will understand the full meaning of the Decalogue.

CHAPTER NINE

The Coming of Age of Neighborly Love

At times, modern man interprets superficially St. Augustine's words "Be mindful of love and do 'as you please.'" Either he hears only the second part of the sentence, "do as you please," or he fails to realize the tremendous implications contained in the first part of the sentence, "Be mindful of love"—that is, have love.

The understanding of the true meaning of love requires constant effort and study even though such knowledge of Christ and the heavenly Father ultimately remains a gift of faith. Anyone knowing the true meaning of love in every situation ranks far above the most learned of modern scholars and scientists. Yet to possess genuine love—to be a loving person is infinitely greater. He who fully understands the meaning of love and its requirements will be receptive to its demands and thereby prove himself mature.

Constant Conversion as the Way to Maturity

Man enters the world not only as a minor but as a stranger in a world of adults and children where there is an ongoing struggle between true and unenlightened love, between unselfish concern and exploitation. Our own heart wavers between the Adamitic self-centered man who sees all things in relation to his ego and the redeemed man who is open to God and respectful of the dignity and uniqueness of his neighbor.

We are enriched through our experience by the genuine

unselfish love of our parents and friends. At the same time, we are bound to experience the hard realities of life and the disappointment of our own limitations and narrow-mindedness.

Both the positive and negative experiences of our life may be used as raw materials for the building blocks of our own future maturity. In a spirit of faith man discerns God's gracious invitation in every circumstance of his life which invites him to reach a decision. Man makes progress on the road to Christian maturity when he accepts himself and when, in the growing awareness of his abilities and limitations, he gathers his forces to overcome the inclinations and tendencies of his own ego. Genuine acceptance of self presupposes acceptance of others despite their limitations and shortcomings. It implies a humble acceptance and recognition of all the good received from them.

Christian maturity includes the humble acceptance of our very lack of maturity, of our limitations and even our sinfulness. Yet it has nothing in common with a fatalistic attitude or any self-complacency. Maturity is a goal to be sought during a lifetime. At the same time, it is a blueprint outlining not only the chief direction or aim but also indicating the various steps along the path towards an ever more perfect maturity. Aware of our limitations and the burden of past neglects, man must know in what direction he is to grow. The decisive word regarding the way and direction should be Christ's own: "I am the Way, the Truth, and the Life" (Jn 14:6).

A Christian who has achieved a certain degree of maturity is not beset and confused by the riddles of life, neither does he possess all the answers in the form of clear-cut directives and precepts. He rather places himself in the presence of Christ, opening his heart and mind to listen. He is able to perceive God's call and invitation even if at times it might be obscure. The Christian, who like Christ centers his life around the will and interest of the heavenly Father's will has truly found direction, strength and personal freedom. On the other hand, the man whose orientation is his own ego, will get lost, confused and paralyzed. Egocentricity makes man unhappy and despondent.

While still on his earthly pilgrimage, man is in need of constant vigilance and effort if he truly wishes to follow Christ. Although man finds his true self-fulfillment in following Christ, he must beware of his arbitrary ego misleading him from his goal-directed striving towards Christ. Vigilance makes man alert to opportunities for good. It also demands that he scrutinize his motives so that his good works may be done in view of Christ whom he truly will see and love in his neighbor; otherwise, man will run the risk of a certain idolatry, of dancing around the golden calf of selfishness.

Christian vigilance derives its strength from a sincere determination to oppose the selfish ego in all its various manifestations, so that man may open himself more and more to the "you" of God and the "we" of neighbor and community. This is basically the meaning of Christian self-denial, mortification or constant conversion.

Two Forms of Personalism

Man's history is characterized by the tension between the image of man as portrayed by Adam and the absolutely mature man represented by Christ Jesus.

Adam and Eve looked away from God, indeed they hid from His sight as soon as they began to worry selfishly about their maturity, their freedom, their wisdom and their self-fulfillment. Eve started her soliloquy with the dark abyss of the selfish self, within which are hidden all the forces of evil. An ego all entangled in itself urges isolation in independence from the "you" of God: "The woman saw that the tree was good to eat and pleasing to the eye, and that it was desirable for the knowledge that it could give; so she took some of its fruit and ate it. Then the eyes of both of them were opened and they realized that they were naked" (Gen 3:6-7).

Adam's personalism is a personalism which turned away from God. It is characterized not only by the fact that Adam and Eve are hiding from God—since He has become a reason for fear, the fear for self-realization and arbitrary maturity—but also by man's overbearing attitude toward the woman: "It was the woman you put with me; she gave me the fruit" (Gen 3:12). In this kind of personalism, man will try to lord over woman (Gen 3:16); he will despise her dignity in polygamy and try to impress her with his audacity and superiority over others (Gen 4:19-24). A personalist filled with the Adamitic desire for a selfish self-fulfillment will associate with the "you" of others, but he will be unable to ultimately find his own "you," because whatever he does, he does only with reference to his own self-glorification. His selfishness will prompt him to desert his partner as soon as it appears that she no longer furthers his desire for elevation and glory.

The Adamitic personalist may not always act as obviously as did Lamech, descendant of Cain and heir to the old urban culture: "Hear my voice, Lamech's wives, listen to what I say: I killed a man for wounding me, a boy for striking me" (Gen 4:23). Such a man can also disguise himself as a moralist who wants to put everything—religion, world and man—into the service of his own self-perfection. Great benefactor that he may be—he might give away all his possessions—but ultimately not for the sake of others, but rather in order to produce the image of a perfect man rich with merits. Perhaps his stoic determination will enable him to subdue his passions, including his capacity for joy—and yet he does this, ultimately, out of a concern for the protection of his own ego, in an ever-increasing incapacity to share happiness and sorrow with others. Hidden beneath his cowl, he may dedicate his life to a contempt for the world for the sake of his own "salvation," both among Buddhists and Christians, without really caring for the wholesomeness of either world or fellow man. He will vie with the zealous Pharisee in observing the law's smallest detail in order to seek in the law his own righteousness, not hearing his fellow man's cries for love and charity, unconcerned with honoring God's wish to reveal Himself as the Father of all.

These personalists will not only fill the pages of history; they will build chairs and pulpits for themselves, they will establish their own schools of philosophy and religion. Some will make frequent use of God, others will deny Him with or without vehemence. But common to them all, despite all differences, is the characteristic of considering everything in soliloquy with their superego, with the serpent of selfish righteousness. In self-chosen isolation, forgetful of the presence of God or man, such a person is concerned only with his personal freedom and status as an adult.

But we probably never will meet such a perfect specimen of this type of a frustrated personalist, a self-made god completely entangled in his own self. In the most remote corner of such a man's heart there somehow still remains the call for the "you" that wants to be taken seriously for its own sake. Somewhere one will hear the cry: "What a wretch I am! Who will save me from this isolationary personalism?" "Thanks be to God through

D

Jesus Christ our Lord!" (Rom 7:24). Christ is the new Adam, the Redeemer of unredeemed personalism as well as of the disorder of modern mass society.

Christ understands Himself and lives as a person coming from and going to the Father, as the messenger of the Father's love anointed by the Holy Spirit to sacrifice Himself for His brothers for the sake of revealing the love of God. "Christ did not think of himself" (Rom 15:3). In the Easter mystery the true victory of self is realized in dedication to the "you." And this is not a mere myth: it is an historical event which makes history, indeed gives ultimate meaning to the whole of history.

Through the grace of God, man can look up to Christ in faith and thus understand his own personality as a call from God. By faithfully listening to Christ's call, the ego opens up to the "you" in the other human beings with the best of its possibilities. The more intensified our belief in Christ becomes, the more receptive we become to the call for reverential and unselfish—and therefore joyful—love and responsibility to our neighbor in the community. As our belief in Christ progresses and deepens, it brings about a progressive openness toward our fellow man unless it is impeded by special psychological and sociological causes.

Accordingly, the commandment of love is not merely added like an ingredient to the decisive condition of a person: it rather expresses and realizes the ultimate and best possibility of the person created in the image of God. The person develops according to the divine plan; he realizes himself in surrendering himself in faith to Christ, which presupposes and produces openness and service to the "you" and to the "we" of the community. The redeemed person finds his true self in the I-you-we relationship after the example of Christ.

In the complexity of life, as well as in the rational efforts of theologians and philosophers, all kinds of transitions are found between the Adamitic person and a personalism that assimilates itself to Christ. We are forever working to overcome selfish personalism and to fulfill our personality in union with Christ.

Readiness and Ability to Take Responsibility

Loving a person as a person is not merely a matter of instinct or blind passion. It is an answer to the gift and call of a love that centers around the "you" rather than the "I." Genuine Christian love and maturity grow with the ability to listen, with empathy and the willingness not to offer a premeditated love to the other human being, but to respond and to serve him in accordance with his reasonable wishes and his willingness to listen to us.

The morality of Christian love is not a pedantic clinging to rules covered with dust, nor is it a playful confidence in our own good intentions. Of course, good intentions and good attitudes are a prerequisite for proper orientation, for the ability to listen. But orientation does not release us from the task of looking intently to the reality and its structures. Christian ethics, is, indeed, an ethics of attitudes and of responsibility.

But such an ethics requires an intimate knowledge of human nature and of the world; a knowledge of our own ego in all its heights and depths; a knowledge of our fellow man and of our environment; a knowledge of the importance of customs and of the structures of law; a knowledge of economy, art and public opinion, to mention only a few. Our actions are not only a manifestation of our sentiments; they are always an encroachment not only on our own history, but also always on the fate of other men. They seep deep into the "you" and "I," and spread out into the construction of an external order which sustains man.

Increasing knowledge about the limits of one's competence, about human nature and the world is a decisive step toward maturity. Willingness to assume responsibility must be measured by the capacity to bear such responsibility. This is particularly true of such fundamental decisions as the choice of a marriage partner, taking up a government position, or beginning a career in journalism. A person with a tendency to faintheartedness and with only a limited knowledge of the psychological facts of life is not acting responsibly if she or he chooses a marriage partner with a marked tendency to get angry very easily or to get drunk.

Man's maturity is a progressive phenomenon; it implies willingness to learn from others, to accept counsel, even to make mistakes . . . as long as one is willing to correct them and to accept the consequences. No man is born either an artist or a scholar; initial failures should not discourage us. Yet it is necessary that we learn early in life to cope with failure. Maturity requires a responsible choice of vocation in view of one's special gifts and talents.

There is a romantic kind of "responsibility ethics" which hardly deserves the name of ethics. It attempts to do away with all rules of social conduct, all the moral laws, thus making the person's solitary decision the sole criterion in a given situation. Even the most gifted man, even the genius stands in need of social rules, of traditional forms of politeness; and in questions of morals, he needs time-honored concepts and the fundamental principles of moral conduct.

Particularly, the child and the adolescent need more than a rational external order. Up to a certain point, they also need the guidance and control of the educator or person in authority. All this should be interpreted as aiming toward a more responsible person. The imperatives must, therefore, not be presented arbitrarily. The yardstick of Christian education and use of authority must not be blind obedience, but insight into a command and above all respect and knowledge of the other person.

Both our pluralistic society and our ever-changing world need the greatest possible number of men who are willing and able to take on responsibility. Otherwise, the society and the world will degenerate into dictatorship and slavish conformity. An attempt to educate with mere imperatives, with laws, rules and statutes, drives the stronger individuals of the younger generation into open rebellion; the danger exists that the weaker ones are being prepared to conform to different attitudes and concepts which these young men and women, who have become unable to act on their own, are bound to confront accidentally at some point in their lives. If 19-year-old Jean, who has learned nothing else at home and in the parish but to be docile and obedient, accidentally runs into gangs, beatniks or rowdies, she very likely will assimilate herself with the same "docility."

Room for Initiative and Freedom

A jet airplane requires quite a long runway. Man, too, needs sufficient room for free initiative—including the possibility of making mistakes. If we are to expect him to grow into a mature and responsible human being, a child or adolescent must have the opportunity to develop his creative talents, particularly in the sphere of morals—that is, in his search for the corresponding expression of genuine charity and responsibility for the "you," for the community and for himself. Therefore, rules and commandments must not be overly strict.

In this regard, a significant correspondence can be

noticed between the psychological requirements for a gradual personal maturity, on the one hand, and on the other, a shift in emphasis from the "border law" to the "target commandment" in the Sermon on the Mount. Life in accordance with the Sermon on the Mount, and particularly under the conditions of life in modern society, calls for a Christian who has a highly developed and deep insight into the nature of the good, the psychic energies, and that initiative and courage needed to take on responsibility.

Education and personal growth in accordance with this ideal is not free of risks. This ideal cannot possibly be achieved without some mistakes. If, however, one stakes everything on legalistic narrow-mindedness and maximum control in order to avoid some of the risks of a morality of love and responsibility, then one has rescued oneself from the risk of life through the choice of death, through a moral suicide. The proper handling of this dilemma calls for facing the risks and aiming at the golden mean. Christian maturity is a goal which can only be approached gradually, a goal for which one must constantly strive by mobilizing all forms of skill and knowledge. The more Christianity is able to produce truly responsible and mature individuals, the more will she also undertake to guarantee human dignity to persons wanting in the psychological and moral spheres.

Fulfilled Existence

Christian religion and morality should not be used for self-aggrandizement or the search for satisfaction and self-fulfillment. A mature Christian loves the good for its own sake, that is, he is open to the "you" and the "we"; he reciprocates love; he gathers all the energies of love particularly when a fellow man is in danger of succumbing due to lack of charity.

However, it is not wrong to keep one's own fulfillment in mind as long as God and one's fellow man are not exploited for selfish reasons, but are loved for their own sake. It is part of our confidence in God and the power of love that, in our dedication to the good, we also expect, ultimately, our own personal fulfillment. But this fulfillment must not be confused with a short-term payment, a remuneration or with self-satisfaction. The good by its nature is equipped with the power to make us happy; yet, it cannot give complete happiness so long as we selfishly search for our ego in our charitable endeavors.

CHAPTER TEN

The Person
in Community and Society

The first general councils of the Church were characterized by their struggle for an adequate expression of the mystery of the Blessed Trinity, particularly the true humanity and divinity of Christ. Today's questions center around man, the human person and the community. If we ask our questions without turning to the mystery of the Divine Persons, then our concern for man can easily lead us into fallacies, even those of atheism. "Some extol man so extravagantly that their faith in God becomes anemic, though they seem more inclined to affirm man than to deny God" (*Pastoral Constitution on the Church in the Modern World*, Art. 19).

In modern philosophy, a personalistic approach predominates. It finds its adherents among all kinds of people, because it corresponds to modern man's basic experiences, to his fears and hopes. Our present generation has seen unscrupulous dictatorships trample human dignity underfoot and turn man into an object of cold-blooded calculation. Mao Tse-tung is joining the ranks of Hitler and Stalin when he asserts that in the case of a war the loss of 100 or 200 million men would not mean much to China.

Human dignity and man's capacity for love are further endangered by a highly structured and impersonal society. A worker who spends eight hours a day on a deadening assembly line, or at other depersonalizing types of work, deeply appreciates the personal relationships in family, marriage, courtship and friendship. Man desires to be more than a mere wheel in a machine, more than a useful member of a functional community. Man, considered only in view of his contribution or used as a mere commodity, feels alienated, threatened and lost. He wants to be recognized and appreciated as a person.

Community with God and Earthly Community

The *Pastoral Constitution on the Church in the Modern World*, in its structure and reasoning, states this expectation of modern man clearly: "Above all the Church knows that her message is in harmony with the most secret desires of the human heart when she champions the dignity of the human vocation, restoring hope to those who have already despaired of anything higher than their present lot. Far from diminishing man, her message brings to his development light, life, and freedom" (*Pastoral Constitution on the Church in the Modern World*, Art. 21).

The decisive aspect in the Church's message remains always the personal communion of man with God: Man is a person, because God calls him personally and because God makes him capable of responding in love. Man fully realizes himself as a person through his acts of love, and a faith inspired by love—a faith which becomes active in fraternal love. Christian morality must seriously involve itself with the full realization of the human community and the earthly society in order to strengthen the genuineness of faith and of personal encounter with God. Not only does faith demand the attitude and act of love, but in many respects, it also builds on human experience in community and society. A genuine communion of love prepares the way for a vital and joyful belief in the God of love.

The man whose experiences are limited to those of a community or society geared and oriented towards selfish goals will likewise tend to envision God in a purely utilitarian way. He will run the risk of seeing Him in the role of a large-scale manager. Such a man will use the sacraments as means and make use of indulgences and religious services with petty calculations towards his own security. His religious vocabulary becomes characterized by utilitarian categories of "means and end." Such an impoverished approach is responsible for producing the priest who acts like a career man and thereby becomes a deterrent of good and a source of unbelief of many.

The father of Karl Marx followed the example of many citizens when he decided to have himself and his entire family baptized in order to promote his business, thereby implanting contempt for religion in the heart of the young Marx. He hated religion which was, on the one hand, a sentimental veil over the stark realities of life, and on the other, a means for worldly gain. His experience in his immediate community barred him from understanding the true meaning of religion as a brotherhood or a community centered around the all-holy and all-loving God.

A petty, despotic and forever nagging father on the one hand, and an intimidated mother on the other, can give rise to an utterly wrong idea of God: the image of their father can influence children throughout their lives in regard to their prayer, their confession and their concept of religion, often manifesting itself in an obsessive-compulsive neurosis or an ultimate denial of God.

God is not merely a product of human fancy. He is our Lord and Creator, whether we recognize Him or not. But the mode of our religious openness, our receptivity, our confidence, our gratitude, even of our visual disturbances and our isolation, depends largely on our experiences in the family community and larger society. This is a cogent reason why we should make every possible effort for well-structured earthly communities. Marriage and the

family should be our primary social concern, but not the
only one.

Family, Society and State

In our daily lives as well as in literature and philosophy,
we frequently encounter a type of "personalism" which
concerns itself only with the immediate personal relationships in marriage, family and friendship while either completely ignoring society and state or merely accepting them
passively or as necessary evils. A similar attitude can be
seen with regard to one's vocation and career—they are
considered only as a means of livelihood, necessary to
raise a family. The proper perspective and relationship between the fundamental personal communities and the social
and political life is of prime importance for the future of
mankind, for the full development of the person and, last
but not least, for the mission of Christians in the world.

The Church will not cease to teach and stress the fact
that the family is the fundamental community, where
man can and should learn the true meaning of love and the
spirit of responsibility. Here we encounter one of the insurmountable contradictions between the Christian and
the classical Marxist view. In Marxism, modern man is a
social being. The end and meaning of education is the
Marxist economic society. Since 1956, roughly seven
million children in the Soviet Union were systematically
raised in the "factory of the new Soviet man" according
to the highly effective psychological methods of the leading
Communist social psychologist, A. S. Makarenko. As early
as the age of three months, the little ones are exposed
to "collective education." From the collective nursery
school to the university, everything is aimed toward dis-

cipline and efficiency of the Soviet citizen. The results are, as the experts tell us, very good: already at the age of 18 months these children can eat and dress all by themselves and are even toilet-trained. At a very early age, they join the group and teach one another; they even criticize one another. In view of their efficiency, their social adaptation, and obedience these children are undoubtedly normal, indeed, frequently better developed than those who grow up within their families. But their emotional life is characterized by a striking deprivation and dependency. It seems that the Red Guards which are such a pliable tool in the hands of Mao likewise received such a kind of education.

Granted that here and there we could learn quite a bit from the psychology of Makarenko, we must nevertheless clearly understand that we cannot aspire to this kind of success. In our view, the man who is a great success in life is not the conformist or the robot, but the man who is capable of love and who lives according to a personal conscience oriented towards and responsive to the fundamental value of love. In that light, the family is normally irreplaceable. There the children learn above all a respect for the "you," a spontaneous and, at the same time, disciplined love. Our best Christian orphanages and reform schools for broken families are guided by this philosophy: the children are brought up in groups which imitate the natural conditions of the family as closely as possible.

On the other hand, the social teachings of the Church do not overlook the fact that the family must be responsive to social and political responsibility. Personalism, in the Christian sense certainly does not mean isolation within the intimate community of the family, but rather a humanization of all the spheres of life in the spirit of love

and respect, initiative and responsiblity, freedom and obedience. These are best learned in the well-ordered atmosphere of a family.

Often enough modern sociology has documented the
interaction between family and society, family and culture,
family and economy, and family and career. The family
as an institution can be healthy only to the extent that
families are aware of their responsibility for the right organization of culture, economy, society and the political order.
Conversely, culture, society and state can truly prosper
and remain human only when they consider themselves
co-responsible for a healthy development of family life.

Man is a unified whole; every attempt at a dichotomy
into a personal and an impersonal sphere destroys the
unity of man. This was also acknowledged to some extent
by Makarenko, even more so than by the many Com-
munists who apply his methods. He emphasizes that parents
and teachers figure prominently in man's development.
Man enters into a variety of personal and social relationships. If we want to become the "salt of the earth," we must
clearly understand the influences for good and evil in the
world around us, particularly the effects of evil influences.
We must work with others to imprint on our world the
stamp of love and responsibility, the stamp of genuine
humanity.

Personalism on Different Levels

Primitive animism not only sees life and spirit in everything;
it is also unable to see the difference between persons,
animals and things. Those who believe in the migration
of the soul would rather let their brothers starve than assent
to the killing of the traditionally holy cows, while a Chris-

tian personalist distinguishes clearly between a person or a community of persons on the one hand, and things, factual processes, biological functions and organism on the other. This does not mean that he is not affected by those things which are not directly an expression of the human person. The love of the Creator and of many men, of entire generations, or the lack of love or responsibility on the part of man, finds expression in everything.

It is the task of the human person to understand— particularly in man but also in everything else—the language of God, the divine spark of the Creator's power, and to use everything in such a way that beyond its temporary usefulness, it also expresses humaneness, justice, goodness, reverence and responsibility. A few examples might shed some light on what we have said so far.

A well cultivated home, be it poor or rich, is more than a mere shelter against the weather; it is not only highly useful economically, but it has affective values, also. It radiates a certain spiritual climate. A home is made comfortable and attractive by the love of those who live in it. The flowers on the table, selected with the husband's taste in mind, are part of the loving reception he meets when he returns from work or from a trip.

A family dinner is more than the feeding of hungry people; it embodies the father's work, the mother's loving care, a feeling of togetherness and tender consideration. The careful preparation of food finds its full response not only in a hearty appetite, but also in the gratitude, the recognition, the consideration for the thoughts and attitudes in it.

A dinner at a hotel may be expensive and superbly prepared; nevertheless, it does not possess the same personal values of a modest meal prepared by a loving wife or mother. This does not mean that we should not think gratefully of those people who serve us and who prepare our meals at the hotel. A friendly and sincere expression of gratitude to the persons waiting on us is part of the humaneness of the meal and of our truly human behavior, even though it does not take on the intimate level of a family meal.

A conversation between engaged or married people is something entirely different from the factual discourse with our employer or the teller who cashes our check. Even though we are on a different level here, we must not forget for a single moment that we are dealing with human beings. A friendly greeting creates an atmosphere of love and respect. An employee in an office or a department store may be unfriendly and peevish today because she does not feel well or because she has been offended by her fiancé or her husband; if my reaction is unfriendly and arrogant, I merely aggravate her problem without being aware of it. However, if I find a word of kindness or have a sense of humor, then perhaps I might even become a peacemaker.

But touching the right note or finding the right word is not enough. We Christians are personalists when we treat our employer and our co-workers justly, and when we perform our work with a feeling of responsibility to all the other persons connected with the business, be he employer or customer. However, if we do our work only in view of the salary or for the sake of our career, we are not Christian personalists in the proper sense of the word, but rather impersonal individualists.

The political arena is not a family affair, nor is it a sports club; the language spoken there is considerably different from that used among classmates or art buffs.

Even in the heat of an argument with a political opponent, the Christian personalist will never forget that his opponent is a person with the right to respect and a good name. A certain nobility which transmits to the neighbor our belief in the sincerity of his intentions—either implicit or explicit—contributes to the humanization of politics and is superior to an objective argument. In addition, a Christian personalist will not forget for a single moment that both in politics and in daily life the well-being of every human person is at stake, not only the mere prestige of a selected few or the power of factions.

A political argument is in many respects different from an argument among theologians or a dialogue between confessor and penitent. Anyone who tries to carry through all three kinds of conversation on just the same level would miss the point. During an argument between theologians it is a matter of the best possible recognition of the truth that God revealed; therefore, it is not enough that theologians say niceties to each other where the truth of salvation may be at stake. But if they turn a theological argument into a personal weapon or an attack against schools of the Church, they betray both truth and personalism. Only when they listen to each other in a spirit of love, when they make an honest effort to understand each other and to express fragmentary insights as humbly and as understandably as possible, only when both partners address each other before God, do they achieve the level proper to them. During confession the dialogue is not a cross-examination, nor a theological lecture, but rather joint praise of God's justice and mercy, a reverent search for the next step on the road to salvation and holiness.

The confessor, the theologian and the politician may be forced to discuss the same subject—for instance the indissolubility of marriage—but each will discuss it with a different vocabulary and on a different level. The confessor may show a wife who firmly believes in the indissolubility of marriage, but who refuses to resume a normal marital life with her husband, that she is practically forcing her husband into divorcing her; he will relate God's forgiveness to her husband's infidelity and thereby point out to her the only possible solution, namely to prove her faithfulness by forgiveness. Such a conversation certainly requires the very special atmosphere of prayer, reverence and compassion.

The theologians will resort to every method offered by historical research and, conscious of the various theological criteria, they will discuss how fundamental faithfulness—faithfulness to the principle of the indissolubility of marriage—might be combined with pastoral benevolence when dealing with people who got into a tricky situation through no or some fault of their own.

The politician, on the other hand, will neither talk like a confessor nor preach like a theologian, but, knowing the mentality and the web of political forces, he will search for the arguments and suggestions that, in our modern world, are apt to contribute to the protection of the stability of marriage and the well-being of the innocent partner and children. He, too, acts like a true personalist: he tries to figure out the thinking of his partners and opponents in order to be able to understand their point of view and to convince them, if necessary, of his own ideas. In addition, he will have a very clear idea about the common good and will envision the welfare of all persons under the law. When he advocates a good piece of family legislation, he knows that he serves not only the abstract idea of the state, but indeed, the living state in view of the greatest well-being of all its citizens.

The Community of Nations

Jesus replied to the lawyer who asked Him "who is my neighbor?" by telling the parable of the Good Samaritan moved with compassion when he came upon the Jew who fell into the hands of brigands (Lk 10:29-37). This was definitely a shock to the Jews, who would not even speak to a Samaritan—especially since the Lord introduced a person from the other side of the fence as showing compassion. Every man can be my neighbor when Divine Providence leads us together and enables us to do good to each other. We all belong to the great family of God. Christ has sacrificed Himself for everybody. As the redeemed we are called to open ourselves to all men as best as we can.

Yet, it would be oversimplifying the idea of personalism if we talked about it only in connection with person-to-person relationships. Considering the steadily increasing social relationships in their ever-growing importance for personal and family life, a Christian personalist will devote himself to the cultivation of good international relations on all possible levels. The breadth of Catholic thinking and believing must be reflected in willingness to accept worldwide responsibility. No one can honestly claim "I believe in the one Catholic Church" unless he identifies himself with the unity of Christianity and of nations within the limits of his position and competence.

The reasons inciting a Christian personalist to become a patriot, for the progress and welfare of his fatherland, will also compel him to do everything in his power to further the community of nations, peace on earth, just international agreements, and an end to hunger in the world through the promotion of developing nations. No Christian can bypass this perspective, especially after the encyclicals

Mater et Magistra and *Pacem in Terris* of Pope John, the peace efforts of Pope Paul, the *Pastoral Constitution on the Church in the Modern World* of the Second Vatican Council as well as several similar resolutions drawn up by the World Council of Churches. This is the proper way of speaking of God, the Creator and Redeemer of all mankind.

CHAPTER ELEVEN

We Are the Church

Many have suffered because of the Church, and indeed, have not known what to make of her. The working class and, generally, the lowest social strata could never understand the showy titles and language of a "higher" clergy that affiliated itself with the higher social classes. The last century brought on the greatest emigration that ever occurred in the history of the Church. One spoke of the Church as dying in men's souls before there was any mention of God's absence from their lives.

There are certainly various reasons for this phenomenon. Pope John and the Council caused the world to take a renewed interest in the Church, an interest unheard of previously. New hopes flared up. The bishops gathered for the Council and professed a program of renewal in humility, in obedience to the Gospels and in docility to the Holy Spirit in accordance with the all-encompassing commandment of love. In spite of initial tensions, a surprisingly broad agreement was reached in the final votes on the models to the various constitutions. After all, what did those 75 votes "not in favor" mean when compared to the 2309 votes "in favor" (December 7, 1965) when the longest and most daring document of the Council was put to the vote? Except for the members of the *Comitato Romano* (an organized group of conservative bishops) everybody held high hopes that the ship of the Church was on her course to new horizons.

Meanwhile, the signs indicate that the ship of Peter will still encounter stormy days, less because of enemies from without than because of tensions that must be re-solved from within. Many observed, with fear and distrust, all the apparent or actual attempts made by a small but powerful conciliar opposition to prove that the Council had met with failure after all. Militant groups of tradi-tionalists organized themselves.

Progressive groups now interpret the helplessness or hesitation of bishops or Church authorities as a secret or open conspiracy with the fanatic traditionalists, a suspicion which, by and large, lacks any foundation. In this climate of distrust, the radicalism of many a "reformer" mush-rooms. Eloquent laymen and priests raise impatient voices in the name of a passionate interest in and love for the Church.

And while the aged Maritain is ostracizing extremists of the Left and prophets of a thorough reform, in a mixture of humor and irony, Charles Davis, a hitherto quiet and circumspect theologian with the highest reputation in the English-speaking world, appears on TV and declares to the world his decision to leave the Church he finds un-loving and corrupt. His starting signal for a "better" Chris-tianity without the Church is—aside from vague charges against the entire Church—a special, far-from-loving in-crimination of the pope.

Only God can pass the final judgment here; He alone knows the entire tragedy of this and many other cases of mistaken people in the Church. The extremists in the reactionary camp certainly have no reason to rejoice, if they are concerned about the Church and not only about proving that they were right all along when they prophesied that "Fifty years would not be enough to rectify all the mistakes of Pope John."

If we love the Church—and we cannot truly love Christ, the Lord of the Church, unless we love His Church

—then we have every reason to ponder our own role. Would Charles Davis ever have been able to pass a judgment so summary, so harsh, unloving and unjust, if he had first examined himself, in everything he suffered because of the Church, according to the principle: We all are the Church? If we begin like outsiders, to stare constantly at the few dozen officials of the Church who have turned apathetic, and if, by looking at them, we take offense at the entire Church, then we have forgotten that we are ourselves a part of the Church; more, we are blindly overlooking the many devoted bishops and priests and all the many genuine Christians.

Christ's Suffering Because of Us—Because of His Church

There is an unchristian way to cope with the imperfections and sins in the Church—we discuss everything with the remark: "Oh well, they are human like everybody else. Why should they be any different?" Even an Alexander VI and his son, Cesare Borgia, born out of wedlock, are accepted, the cardinal and captain of brigands; for "they were products of their time." We are annoyed with senile prelates who desperately try to hold on to their offices chiefly because such conduct is no longer fashionable in our modern, business-oriented society.

This attitude is no less a betrayal of the Church than the anguished cry of Charles Davis. Christ has suffered because of the temporal thinking of His Apostles and disciples. He spoke harshly to Peter who dared try to talk Him out of His desire to suffer and die for His people (Mt 16:21-23), and who declared, sure of himself, that he would not lose faith even when all the others might (Mt 26:33-35). His sleepy Apostles were a special source of suffering to the Lord on the Mount of Olives.

If we believe in the mystery of the Church and then see how traditionalists keep systematically aloof, concerning themselves only with their own ideas and fighting each other in full view of the pentecostal storm of the Second Vatican Council, then this must be a source of deep suffering to us. But we must not scream with fear as if the Lord were not present on the ship anymore. We must not overlook all the good aspects of the Church, her openness in order, her order in openness, her honest search and scrutiny, and the holy lives of so many simple believers, religious, priests and bishops.

If we believe that the entire people of God is called to sanctity, we will not merely accuse prelates and theologains, but above all, we will feel the pangs of our own contribution and humbly confess our own failures.

We Are the Church of Sinners

The overly zealous servants who wanted to weed out the darnel sprouting with the new wheat would have thoroughly trampled down the field and the entire seed. They are not only like those priests who, in their relentless rigorism —particularly in matters which are not part of the unchanging laws of God—have driven many out of the Church or, indeed, have barred them from receiving the sacraments; they are also like those impatient theologians and laymen who, in their zeal for reform, are pulling the authority of the Church to pieces.

If our Lord were faced with the bitter criticism of bishops and priests who seem either too flexible or too narrow-minded, would He not call these modern executioners to account by saying, "If there is one of you who has not sinned, let him be the first to throw a stone" (Jn 8:8)?

In an age like ours, criticism cannot be avoided. But criticism can serve as a cleanser, as a basis for building, only when it is inspired by love and uttered in a spirit of humility. Even when controversies and criticisms arise— criticism of certain attitudes and opinions which, in our way of thinking, are wrong and even dangerous—we must not forget that we all expect our salvation from God's mercy only. Those who are eager to hasten the eschatological separation of the "sheep from the goats," and who do not hesitate to count others among the goats and themselves among the sheep, must face the worst final disappointment.

But in this time of transition we must be able to judge for ourselves whose example we ought to follow, and whose word we may heed. We must listen to both warnings of the Sermon on the Mount: "Do not judge, and you will not be judged; because the judgments you give are the judgments you will get" (Mt 7:1-2) and "Beware of false prophets. . . . You will be able to tell them by their fruits" (Mt 7:15-16).

We may always hope that failures and/or errors that seem obvious to us are not serious—or, at least, not so serious in God's eyes as man might think. But it is only prudent and in accordance with the Church's teachings for us to be somewhat suspicious and critical of a prelate who, at the Council, fought against the very points which the world's bishops and the successor to Peter taught and promulgated in almost any question, and who then continues to criticize the Council instead of himself, and who declares that nobody should expect him to "change anything which has to do with the way he is and has to be in obedience to the will of God."

A bishop is the official announcer of the gospel in his

diocese and he is the servant of unity; but if he seeks to prevent his priests from applying the Good News of active love to the poor and the discriminated, if he opposes other matters in obvious contradiction to his service to his colleagues and to unity, then all Christians must be firmly determined to force him to correct his errors. Here it is that mature Christians are tested on their ability to combine humility with firmness and respect with criticism in their discernment of spirits.

If we criticize those who confuse authoritarian conduct with Christ's mission and prejudiced personal opinions with Gospel, then we must search our own egos just as thoroughly, asking whether we have not indulged openly or secretly in such temptations ourselves. All our criticism is destructive unless we first feel our own contrition, being conscious at every instant that we belong to the Church of sinners and that we take part in the Church's calling to sanctity according to the degree of our humility.

The Teaching Church and the Listening Church

The Church both "upholds the truth and keeps it safe" (I Tim 3:15). Particularly at a time when everything is in a state of change, we can feel how helpless we would be, in many questions concerning life, if the Church were not our spiritual guide. Christ never ceases to announce the Good News to us and to teach us the truth of salvation through the services of the Church. Christ, who ascended into heaven, pervades the Church with His presence. He bestows on her the promised Spirit of truth; He is the teacher of all men.

All the members of the Church, from the pope down to the child who listened to Jesus' message on his mother's lap, are above all part of the "listening Church"; they are listeners to the Word of God. The Church's teachership is entirely founded on docility. A certain person becomes an authentic teacher in the fullest sense of the word not by holding an office in the Church, but rather by being docile to the utmost, that is, docile to all the different forms through which God teaches us: through Holy Scripture, through the living tradition of the Church, through study of the great theologians, through listening to the wisdom of the humble and the insignificant, through esteem for the religiousness of simple people and of the educated, through attention to the signs of the age, through the example of saints and the virtues of anonymous Christians —and, indeed, of unbelievers—through such scientific achievement of our time as historical research, psychology and sociology.

Genuine docility is to be learned on one's knees, in prayer and confidence in God's grace. Everyone should learn from everyone else, and according to God's way of acting in others. "Each one of us, however, has been given his own share of grace, given as Christ allotted it. . . . And to some, his gift was that they should be apostles; to some, prophets; to some, evangelists; to some, pastors and teachers; so that the saints unite in the work of service, building up the body of Christ. In this way we are all to come to unity in our faith and in our knowledge of the Son of God, until we become the perfect Man, fully mature with the fullness of Christ himself" (Eph 4:7-13). In these words of St. Paul the invaluable gift which the magisterium of the Church represents to us becomes discernible. At the same time it is obviously wrong to dichotomize the Church into a teaching and a learning Church.

To be sure, we are not all the "teaching Church." But we all contribute, either for richness or for impoverishment, in the recognition of truth.

The pope is the supreme teacher of the Church. We owe him special obedience and gratitude. The entire Church must pray to the Holy Spirit for his enlightenment and strength. This does not mean, however, that the pope is not expected to show the highest degree of openness and docility. He is assisted by the Holy Spirit in a very special way, particularly in the few historical moments of a solemn proclamation of a universally binding article of faith; but he does not receive the word directly from the Holy Spirit. That is why the fruitfulness of papal authority is all the greater the more the pope can properly share in the wisdom and experience of the entire assembly of bishops, in the knowledgeability of theologians of all schools of thought, in the experience of laymen from many fields and cultures. The popes somehow have always been the "learning" Church, a fact which was painfully obvious when only a few men with a certain fixed way of thinking were the popes' counsellors.

The bishops' teaching authority increases as a function of their docility to the Holy Spirit, exploring every possibility to participate in the fullness of the Church, in all the forms of collegiality, in all directions.

The pope teaches with the charism of infallibility only in very unusual moments. Though we owe special docility to his entire activity as the teacher of Christianity, it would be unfair to the uniqueness of the act of faith that the faithful be expected to believe and accept every single utterance of a pope as final and irreformable. We are expected to "acknowledge with reverence and adhere sincerely to the judgments made by him according to his manifest mind and will" (*Constitution on the Church*, Art. 24).

A thorough examination of the documents of the First

and Second Vatican Councils permits the theological opinion that the pope is not infallible in questions of mere natural law unless an added aspect of the truth of supernatural revelation is involved. "This infallibility with which the divine Redeemer willed His Church to be endowed in defining a doctrine of faith and morals extends as far as the deposit of divine revelation, which must be religiously guarded and faithfully expounded" (*Constitution on the Church*, Art. 25).

In my opinion, for instance, the encyclical *Casti Connubii* of Pope Pius XI is not a document that can claim infallibility and irreformable finality. This, however, does not mean that we may simply ignore this encyclical. It contains articles of doctrine that cannot be questioned by anyone without giving full license to dangerous errors; for instance, the reference to matrimony as a divine institution, and the relation of married love to the dignified continuation of life, the dignity of the marital act, the inviolability of unborn life, the absolute obligation to faithfulness because of the marriage bond. Furthermore, the duty and right of the Church as teacher—and particularly of the pope—to guard and recognize these principles must be beyond any doubt.

Discussions presently going on among theologians and the laity concern questions of the application of those principles to a situation that is entirely new in many respects. It is a matter of working out formulations which take into account the novelty of the circumstances and the progress made in various branches of science. If progress without discontinuity is understood and expressed properly today, this is mainly due to the sometimes heroic obedience of numerous couples to the teachings of *Casti Connubii* and to the honest, humble efforts of theologians to expound loyally the same teachings in the light of the whole of tradition and with a view to the needs and dangers of marriage in our modern age.

Infallibility in every possible question is by no means a necessary prerequisite of authority and obedience. Parents never possess the charism of infallibility and yet they have authority. To be sure, the extent of their authority depends on the degree of their maturity, their understanding and humility. The Church does not need to be infallible in matters of natural morality so long as morality is not at odds with divine revelation. In questions of salvation and human wholesomeness, we are sufficiently protected and enlightened, if in matters of natural law, the Church gives us directions which exhaust the present possibilities of knowledge without contradicting divine revelation.

The entire people of God—pope, bishops, priests and laity—must, however, remain continually open to a deeper understanding of revelation, to the unfolding of dogmas and particularly to a deeper understanding of those aspects of moral life which are accessible to reason (natural law).

At a time when humanity is confronted with so many new insights, developments and revolutionary changes, new tasks arise particularly for theology and for the proclamation of the truth of faith and natural morality. To avoid the issue and merely repeat what has been traditionally recognized would mean to betray the gospel and to epitomize the bad news of "God is dead." The venture of a searching theology, forever new, can be carried on successfully only in prayer, in solidarity with the entire people of God and in reverent obedience to the authority of the successors to the Apostles. I often wonder, however, why we do not pray more often for theologians; criticism is not enough.

The Second Vatican Council has scrutinized these problems with the vigor peculiar to it, above all in its

Pastoral Constitution on the Church: "From the beginning of her history, she has learned to express the message of Christ with the help of the ideas and terminology of various peoples, and has tried to clarify it with the wisdom of philosophers, too. Her purpose has been to adapt the gospel to the grasp of all as well as to the needs of the learned insofar as such was appropriate. Indeed, this accommodated preaching of the revealed Word ought to remain the law of all evangelization. For thus each nation develops the ability to express Christ's message in its own way. At the same time, a living exchange is fostered between the Church and the diverse cultures of people. To promote such an exchange, the Church requires special help, particularly in our day, when things are changing very rapidly and the ways of thinking are exceedingly various. She must rely on those who live in the world, are versed in different institutions and specialties, and grasp their innermost significance in the eyes of both believers and unbelivers. With the help of the Holy Spirit, it is the task of the entire People of God, especially pastors and theologians, to hear, distinguish, interpret the many voices of our age, and to judge them in the light of the divine Word. In this way, revealed truth can always be more deeply penetrated, better understood, and set forth to greater advantage" (*Constitution on the Church in the Modern World*, Art. 44).

The Sacrament of Love and Unity

The Church's great mission and Christ's prayer for it are the same: "May they all be one. Father, may they be one in us, as you are in me and I am in you, so that the world may believe it was you who sent me" (Jn 17:21). The community of disciples can be the "salt of the earth" and the "light of the world" only to the extent of their striving humbly and repentantly for unity. "By her relationship with Christ, the Church is a kind of sacrament or sign of intimate union with God, and of the unity of all mankind. She is also an instrument for the achievement of such union and unity" (*Constitution on the Church,* Art. 1).

A sacrament is intelligible and, thus, a sign calling on faith and conscience. When the sacramental sign, the sacramental message, is distorted or falsified into its opposite, we do not have a genuine sacrament anymore; it is no longer an instrument of salvation. Wherever the Church fulfills truth in a spirit of love she helps to draw men closer to God and to lead them to a greater unity and love of one another. But when "truth" is used as a weapon against one another, or when, because of personal ambition, it is used as a career tool to kindle dissension or indulge in group egoism, there the "sacrament" of Satan is at work.

Christian communities which feel quite comfortable as separate brothers in their separate "homes," who mock one another and are not willing to cooperate for the benefit of suffering mankind, do not live the "sacrament of unity." By engaging in such behavior, they refuse to be intelligible signs of unity.

It is the purpose of the Church's laws to protect her unity and openness to the signs of the times, her mission as an intelligible sign of unity. Anyone who insists on clinging to habits or legal regulations after they have ceased to be a protection of vigilant love and a sign and testimony for the Living God of love stymies the Church's true effectiveness.

On the other hand, anyone who, in the midst of the tensions and anxieties of our times, does everything in his power to strengthen loving unity in truth and genuine unity in love, or who reinstates them, is truly the Church.

CHAPTER TWELVE

The Christian
in Marriage and Family

The family is the prototype and smallest unit of the Church. The Church on earth and the "heavenly Jerusalem" are both referred to as the "family of God." The family is the place where religion and life are either integrated or condemned to hopeless separation.

One of the greatest dangers of our age is precisely this cleavage between religion and life; as a result, religion and morality, too, are on the decline. The sad news that "God is dying" in the souls of men is preceded by a moralism which loosely runs parallel to religion and a certain piety which retreats more and more from actual life. A renewed vigor of religion in the hearts of men has its mainspring in the Christian family, which is conscious of its leading role in the social and religious spheres.

The Meaning of the Sacrament of Matrimony

At times, canonists and moralists have discussed the sacrament of Matrimony in a way which has erected a wall between modern man's concept of marriage and its description in Canon Law. Such an error also leads to a misunderstanding of marriage in relation to God's will. Many held the opinion that the valid marriage contract itself, as such, constituted the sacrament and, in a one-sided fashion, emphasized the juridical aspects of a valid "contract." All the obligations and purposes of marriage were enumerated, and it was declared that the contract, since it was a sacrament, bestowed grace of itself (*ex opere operato*) so that married people are able to fulfill their duties.

Among the obligations stressed was the requirement that partners in a marriage love one another in a "supernatural way"; thereby conjugal love was considered merely incidental, but not the essential end of marriage. On the other hand, the reaction among both Catholics and Protestants is a denial of this kind of sacramentality of marriage.

Faithful to the Holy Scripture and the best of Catholic tradition, the Second Vatican Council offers a much more realistic view of the sacrament of Matrimony. The Council text that concerns itself with the holiness of marriage and of the family characteristically begins with the words: "The intimate partnership of married life and love" (*Pastoral Constitution on the Church in the Modern World*, Art. 48). The word contract is purposely omitted. The bond of marriage is discussed as a *covenant* of irrevocable personal consent. It is not a matter of an impersonal nature relating to duties and law, but rather an indissoluble covenant between two persons, a covenant originating in a free act and which, in its essence, is love in the reciprocal giving of the spouses.

The grace of marriage is not merely God's assistance in the duties and obligatons; it is a gift of the powerful works of God's love. It is the special grace of marriage that God calls two human beings to the mutual gift of love and that He makes them capable of loving each other truly and with an ever greater maturity in their role as parents. The grace of marriage is a gift of God's love, and therefore a calling to genuine love. It is "activated" and becomes fruitful, only to the extent that the partner truly reciprocates in love and thus helps the other to a greater love and fidelity. Grace is finally absent in a marriage where the husband and wife fail to work together in order to increase their love, because the specific grace of their vocation has not met with their response.

The meaning of sacrament is: God's saving presence and healing love. The sincerity of the partner's mutual and ever increasing love and devotion draws Christ's powerful presence. According to the measure of their love they experience this salvific presence.

By virtue of the sincerity of their mutual love they are united in the name of Christ, the Redeemer. "Christ the Lord abundantly blessed this many-faceted love, welling up as it does from the fountain of divine love and structured as it is on the model of His union with the Church. For as the God of old made Himself present to His people through a covenant of love and fidelity, so now the Savior of men and the Spouse of the Church comes into the lives of married Christians through the sacrament of Matrimony. He abides with them thereafter so that, just as He loved the Church and handed Himself over on her behalf, the spouses may love each other with perpetual fidelity through mutual self-bestowal" (*Pastoral Constitution on the Church in the Modern World*, Art. 48).

It is the special grace and mission of the sacrament of Matrimony that the spouses, through their mutual love, prepare each other for a more meaningful and vital experience of God's love and a more effective love of neighbor. In the first place, the spouses are called upon to love each other deeply and steadfastly; then they will become increasingly able to love their children and to rear them. They will realize: "How rewarding and great must God's love be if man already finds such joy in love! How patient is God's love, because we already manage to be patient, understanding, and forgiving!" Grace bears fruit as soon as married people sense the infinite greatness of God's love for their children, when they strive ceaselessly to deepen this experience through their own love. Each mission implies a special grace. Each command and mission pre-supposes the respective grace to carry out God's design. In Matrimony, the one great commandment—yet more than a commandment in the restricted sense—is that of love. It is a commandment to the extent that we have received and continue to receive more love, the more grate-fully we reciprocate it.

Married Love is Not a Secondary End

The emphasis which the Council and contemporary theol-ogy place on conjugal love is, essentially, as old as divine revelation. Man and woman are made for each other so that—both together and individually—they are an image of God, capable of love. The Bible particularly illustrates this in a parable as intelligible to primitive men as to those familiar with modern depth psychology. Eve is created from Adam's rib—that is, she is his true reflection and corresponds to the innermost desires of his heart. Adam rejoices, therefore, at the sight of the gift which God bestowed on him in woman: "This at last is bone from my bones, and flesh from my flesh! This is to be called woman, for this was taken from man. This is why a man leaves his father and mother and joins himself to his wife, and they become one body" (Gen 2:23-23).

God compares His love for His people with a husband's love for his wife. The Song of Songs, is one of the most intimate love between bride and bridegroom, a song of conjugal love and a praise of God's love. The Council of Trent sums up the essence of traditional thinking on mat-rimony when it teaches that "Christ himself, who instituted the holy sacraments and brought them to perfection, merited for us by his passion the grace that brings natural love to perfection and strengthens the indissoluble unity, and sanctifies the spouses" (*The Church Teaches*—Documents of the Church in English Translation, sixth printing, St. Louis: B. Herder Book Co., 1964. No. 855, p. 336).

The emphasis on married love as the essence of matrimony, however, is new in several respects:

1) Sin darkens conjugal love. The curse of sin above all affected marriage. Adam and Eve became mutually guilty of sin. They did not receive each other and their togetherness from God in a spirit of humble adoration. Consequently Adam's contempt: "It was the woman you put with me..." (Gen 3:12). Sin is reflected in polygamy (Gen 4:19-24), in man's thirst for power over woman, in the double standard which permitted a man the very licentiousness and infidelity he forbade in woman. A change was brought about through the Good News of redemption, particularly with respect to the relationship between the sexes. A man experiences the grace of redemption when he ceases to domineer over his wife and begins to love her with the unselfish love with which Christ loved His Church (Eph 5:25). In a patriarchal social milieu, a woman lived the mystery of salvation to its fullest when she fulfilled her role with humility and love. But the more deeply redemption affects the entire life, the more woman's complete equality and dignity are recognized in the partnership of marriage. Redemption will be felt, again and again, as the completely new sound and accent of love.

2) The social and economic conditions of past centuries often clouded the meaning of conjugal love. The absolutism of princes was largely reflected in the position of the male as the head of the family. Family interests, and frequently

mere economic considerations, determined the choice of marriage partners, to such an extent that frequently the heads of families chose the marriage partner for their child and bargained about the "marriage contract." Although the marriage contract somehow included the core of matrimony, its obvious purpose often was above all a business transaction between two families. Today, at least in the Western world, the choice of partner is the fundamental right of young people. The families may actively counsel as long as they do not endanger the young people's freedom of choice. Moreover the choice of a partner no longer affects the economic and social interests of the two families as it did in past centuries. Thus, conjugal love comes to prominence.

3) In past centuries, life was normally restricted to the more intimate family, with several generations living together. Interpersonal relationships had a determining role due to the close interdependence of the economic and social structures. Modern man, on the other hand, spends a large part of his life in the anonymous realm of today's mass society and impersonal business world. In such a social atmosphere, man feels himself only partially fulfilled as a person. Personal friendship and, above all, the intimate realm of marriage and family assume new importance. Thus, modern personalism, particularly in a form emphasizing the I-you-we relationship, is an expression of the new approach to life—which, to be sure, allows for a variety of realizations running from a superficial sentimentalism to the most mature forms of cheerful and self-sacrificing mutual dedication.

4) Formerly, couples desired the highest possible number of children, even though they might not have loved each other too much. A great number of children meant

economic and social status and the only possible form of old-age insurance. Of course, a good education, even in those days, was possible only when both parents truly loved each other. Today, economic and social considerations tempt the egoist to drastically limit the size of his family. It is getting more and more obvious that, under the new conditions of life, only the most devoted conjugal love is an effective motive to have as many children as one can properly raise and educate.

5) In view of today's knowledge of the Bible, of modern psychology and anthropology, the previously held opinion that the marital act has fundamentally no purpose other than begetting children is untenable and scandalous. It is acknowledged more and more that the full expression of the conjugal union is one of the foundations of the human "word"—an expression of an irrevocable oneness. It has reference, therefore, to fruitfulness in the fullest human sense. Presenting, as alternatives, either having a child or indulging in mere selfish lust has always been a deplorable misunderstanding of the marital act. Today, it is getting increasingly clearer that such an attitude is inhuman and unchristian. Many times, prolonged and forcefully kept total abstinence, together with negligence of marital tenderness, not only provokes grave temptations against marital fidelity (Cf I Cor 7:5), but often enough causes tensions and aggressiveness in one or both partners; via subconscious channels, it often turns into something like "psychological sterilization." One need only think of a young mother who concentrates all her affection on her baby while, misunderstanding marital chastity, she refuses signs of affection to her husband. The husband, then, will unconsciously develop a tendency to avoid another such rival for the affection and attentions of his wife.

Children are no Incidental Matter

The marital calling is, essentially, a calling to parenthood; but surely, this does not imply that a marriage is meaningless or even cursed when it is not blessed with children. Emphatically the Council said: "Marriage, to be sure, is not instituted solely for procreation. . . . Therefore, marriage persists as a whole manner and communion of life, and maintains its value and indissolubility, even when offspring are lacking—despite, rather often, the very intense desire of the couple" (*Pastoral Constitution on the Church in the Modern World*, Art. 50). Conjugal love is in itself a praise of God's love and a high value in itself; but it is also necessary with respect to the parents' love for their children. As partners in the care and love for their children and in reciprocating their children's love, the husband and wife will grow in mutual affection and esteem. Their physical oneness, likewise—even when it is not actually for the purpose of awakening new life—receives a special fullness and dignity in view of their parental calling.

The True Face of Love

In a fundamentally Christian perspective, it is not correct to say that other virtues besides love are necessary in marriage. Everything else, if it is genuinely felt, does not stand in addition to married love, but is rather an expression of genuine love.

Genuine love between the spouses is strong, sincere and tender. It is respectful and considerate, benevolent and grateful; joyous, unselfish and ready to make sacrifices; for that very reason it is itself a fountain of joy; it is gentle and grateful for forbearance, faithful and considerate to make fidelity easy for the partner. It cannot be embittered. It rejoices in the truth which they recognize together and make more accessible to one another. "Love ... is always ready to excuse, to trust, to hope, and to endure whatever comes" (I Cor 13:7). Married love is the source of fruitfulness. It experiences its blessing in the harmonious education of children who, to that love, owe not only their lives, but also their capacity to love and to do good.

Christian love proves its worth in forgiveness. One of the greatest injustices one spouse can commit against the other is infidelity; but the innocent partner will make a humble examination of his own conscience to see whether he or she is not coresponsible for the guilt of the other—it may be due to a lack of tender consideration, a refusal of affection.

Great love will always prevail. It knows how to pray and live according to the words of the Our Father: "Forgive us our trespasses as we forgive those who trespassed against us." God's faithfulness manifests itself in forgiveness. Forgiving love—which itself asks humbly for forgiveness, even where the evidence indicates that one's own guilt is of a lesser degree—celebrates the greatest triumphs on earth and wins the final victory for all eternity.

The love of the redeemed is redeeming love—a love which is salvific in imitation and collaboration with the Redeemer's love for all His brothers and sisters. Sanctified by the sacrament, conjugal love and love for one's children receive a special calling to reciprocal helpfulness along the road to salvation.

Yet, concern for salvation must be neither an adjunct to conjugal love nor a bare, optional superstructure, much less a substitute for loving kindness, understanding and tenderness. The "pious" wife who keeps her husband emotionally starved, who neglects both home and kitchen, adds to the disaster if she lectures to him on religion and virtue. However, a few words about God from a loving wife will bear fruit.

The grace of the sacrament of Matrimony becomes a great blessing for the children, if their parents have truly learned to love each other increasingly through all the vicissitudes of life, and if, in unison, they have manifested the true face of love to their children.

CHAPTER THIRTEEN

Responsible Parenthood

Our grandparents or at least our great-grandparents expressed their faith and their confidence in Divine Providence with the expression: "Children are accepted as God sends them" or "What God sends is well provided for." There was nothing wrong with this attitude. In those days, the pace of life was much slower and people were not as worried about life in general as we are today. There was a time when man cultivated neither a garden nor a field. Then followed many thousands of years of simple hoe cultivation, and then, many years of primitive agriculture. Our modern scientific agriculture is something completely new and different in comparison to the preceding eras. Already, nations must plan ahead together seeking ways to feed the world's population. Not only would return to the level of the primitive fruit gatherer but also return to unscientific agriculture mean nothing less than mass suicide of humanity. However, this is not to say that there would not still be families in a few remote areas of Africa or even of the Abruzzi trying to survive with the methods of pre-scientific agriculture.

It is not arbitrariness, but rather the result of the radical changes in the life of man, in his biological condition, his psychological reactions, his tasks and his knowledge that prompt spouses to ask themselves in all honesty whether they may have another child. If, two or three generations ago, one desired about five adult children, then in view of the high infant mortality rate in those days, one had to aim at about fifteen births. Most children did not need any vocational training; very early, they made themselves useful around a farm or the workshop of an artisan. Rarely did a doctor dare to predict that a new pregnancy would imperil the life of the mother. One simply did not ask this question. It just did not seem to belong to the realm of human responsibility. Today, parents who would expect about fifteen births, providing a relatively early marriage and normal fertility, have to take stock of themselves, asking whether or not they will be in a position to provide these children with an adequate education.

In contemporary U.S.A., about one-third of the younger generation receives a college education. The fact that the American Negro has not yet had the same chances to benefit from the educational boom poses one of the most serious social problems. Similarly, the fact that only about three percent of the population in Latin America receives a college education forestalls a quick socio-economic development so necessary to meet the rapidly increasing population.

"Where does that leave the belief in Divine Providence?"

During a committee meeting where responsible parenthood was the main topic, a pious old archbishop jumped up like an Old Testament prophet and shouted: "Where does that leave your belief in Divine Providence? Have you not read: '. . . I am telling you not to worry about your life and what you are to eat, nor about your body and how you are to clothe it. Surely, life means more than food, and the body more than clothing! Look at the birds in the sky. They do not sow or reap or gather into barns; yet your heavenly Father feeds them. Are you not worth much more than they are?'" (Mt 6:25-26). What about the normative value of the Sermon on the Mount?

If Christ and the Apostles were living today, they would certainly preach the same religious truths, but neither with the same words and parables nor with the same culture in mind. It will always be true that the disciple of Christ is not to give in to chronic worry. But he can no longer afford to dream of a Sabbath year during which there will be neither sowing nor reaping. Today we are no less in the hands of Divine Providence than those people at the time of the Sermon on the Mount. However, Divine Providence has entrusted us with different insights and means. If we do our share and make responsible use of the means by planning and foresight, then we can leave the rest up to the hand of Providence. Whatever may come, it will turn into something good for those who love God. But if we simply twiddle our thumbs, then we are sinning against Divine Providence.

When I nursed patients suffering from typhoid fever during the spring and summer of 1944 in the Pripet Marshes of Russia, when I vaccinated the people and separated the wells for the healthy from those of the sick, I heard the orthodox say: "This priest loves us; but who knows whether he has the right faith; he does not seem to believe that sickness is sent by God and does not come out of wells or toilets!" These pious old farmers from the Pripet Marshes and that pious archbishop from Sicily express their faith in a language, imagination and limitation of human responsibility which is anything but fitting in this scientific era. They believe in God, but only in a God who ruled the prescientific world, not in the God of history who leads mankind through different stages and who demands man's full cooperation in accordance with a specific stage of knowledge and needs.

As long as a husband was unable to have any idea about the dangers involved in a new pregnancy for his wife, he was justified in not feeling guilty when his wife either died or became mentally ill. However, if today he is told by a competent gynecologist, "Your wife needs at least two years of rest unless you want to endanger her health," then a serious question of conscience arises on the basis of this information. If he ignores these warnings, and if, then, his wife winds up in a mental institution with a serious case of post-partum psychosis, he cannot blame Divine Providence. It was this very Providence which enabled him to understand the seriousness of the situation.

The Second Vatican Council points out to modern man how he must adjust himself to Divine Providence in marriage: "Parents should regard as their proper mission the task of transmitting human life and educating those to whom it has been transmitted. They should realize that they are thereby cooperators with the love of God the Creator, and are, so to speak, the interpreters of that love" (*Pastoral Constitution on the Church in the Modern World*, Art. 50). Any arbitrariness must be excluded from the deliberations of responsible parenthood. Yet this is not to say that parents, who are solely competent to decide on the desirable number of children, should not allow a certain leeway for freedom of judgment, for more or less courageous ventures.

The Christian and the New Consciousness

Modern city planning and modern scientific agriculture are challenges to both the believer and the unbeliever. One does not have to remain on the level of primitive fruit gathering or of simple hoe cultivation in order to be faithful. To be sure, the Christian will have additional thoughts about city planning as soon as he realizes how much depends on cultured living for the development of personality and morality.

Similarly, the modern consciousness in view of the transmission of human life is, on a certain level of development, common to both believer and unbeliever. Both decide on the proper time, on the desirable intervals between individual pregnancies. It becomes a matter of conscious decision. The superficial, practical-minded unbeliever will degrade this decision to a mere calculation: "Should we have another child this year or should we buy a color TV set or a new car?" Truly faithful and mature married couples, however, respond to a divine calling in their considerate decision to transmit new life and to raise a child properly. They consider themselves cooperators with the love of the Creator. Their decision assumes the character of a loving response to God, a loving answer to the desires and genuine possibilities of the spouses and the entire family. They will not once and for all set the limits early in their married life: two children—that is it. They will keep themselves forever open for the gifts of the divine love. If their conjugal love, their harmony, their skill in rearing children, and their delight in one another and in their children grow, then their spontaneous gratitude to God will frequently be expressed in their desire for another child.

Modern equalitarianism likes to predetermine how many children one ought to have: "Two, three at the most." Birth control at any price, with the idea of keeping all families small, frequently originates among the privileged classes; they are afraid that their high living standard might somehow be imperiled by the fertility of the masses.

They are opposed to foreign aid and preach, therefore—at a considerable cost—drastic methods of birth planning to the rapidly developing nations of Asia and Africa.

The responsible parenthood of faithful and mature Christians shares only the consciousness of the attitude to these questions with the advocates of birth control and equalitarian birth planning. The mental set and its moral result, however, are as different as night and day. In no way is a Christian always under the obligation to have many children. A mother of one child who has suffered several miscarriages really has risked much and has done the maximum. Others, even after the eighth or ninth child, might still desire another one without being determined that this should be the last one. The Second Vatican Council clearly favors consciously responsible parenthood and praises the family with many children; however, it is encouraged provided that it be the result of a "wise and common deliberation." The parents must also be in a position to suitably bring up even a relatively large family (*Pastoral Constitution on the Church in the Modern World,* Art. 50). Well-raised and well-educated children surely will not aggravate the population problem.

The moment that can transmit new life is transformed into a moment of generous decision for responsible parents when they accept the ensuing sacrifices and restrictive measures; at the same time, it will also be the source of many joys for a good many years. The transmission of human life possesses no intrinsic moral value unless it expresses the acceptance of the totality of the parental calling. It devolves upon the parents to bring up their children to be responsible and mature citizens of the world and the Church. In a pluralistic and highly differentiated dynamic society where practically everything undergoes constant change, rearing children requires much greater skill than was called for with the static and closed social conditions of the past. Thus the concept of "responsible parenthood" includes the added duty of preparing oneself thoroughly, the duty of acquiring—both before and during the years of marriage—the needed pedagogical knowledge. The Christian Family Movement and similar family groups figure prominently in this respect, for there, ideally-minded families share on a small scale their counsel, encouragement, and help.

Birth Control—But How?

Consciously responsible procreation poses the question of how to control birth. This issue is disputed no less hotly but certainly no more than other issues in the course of history: no more than the question of the justification of torture when it was still practiced by the Inquisition, the question related to the burning of "witches" after a papal bull insisted upon it, the question of direct power of the Church in the temporal (political) realm, of the question of usury after the modern economic reform re-evaluated the lending of money in accordance with its new meaning and function. Both moral theologians and believers will probably be confronted with new problematic questions again and again until the second advent of Christ. It is true because of human history which "e pur si muove" (And yet it moves—Galileo) and because there will always be those among us who would rather see the world not move at all. Galileo and his opponents will not have to complain about a lack of successors.

The current discussions going on in the Church are rather confusing to many. That is why some people would have theologians remain silent. Undoubtedly, this would be the most convenient solution; indeed! Yet, is this responsible in view of the din of the media of mass communications: radio, newspapers, films and everyday discussions? It is the principal task of the theologian to study these questions thoroughly, to discuss them with experts, to listen to the laymen, especially those known for their particular competency in certain scientific fields. Yet, since this issue is debated on every street corner and every wave length, and since some Christians might arrive at the most dangerous conclusion that everything has become doubtful, it is the duty of the theologian to state the argument clearly, delineating—in the essential aspects—what is not up for discussion, at least insofar as Catholic theology is concerned.

The sacred right to life of every human being is beyond any debate. "Therefore from the moment of its conception, life must be guarded with the greatest care, while abortion and infanticide are unspeakable crimes" (*Pastoral Constitution on the Church in the Modern World*, Art. 51). The dilemma of the moral theologian consists only in the fact that there do, indeed, exist certain borderline cases in which everything must be done to save the lives of both mother and child. An operation is not to be called an abortion in the strict moral sense (does not deprive the child of its right to life) if a competent obstetrician, in his function as the interpreter of Divine Providence, determines that the child, having no chance to survive, must die whereas the life of the mother, however, can still be saved. These extreme cases have become fewer and fewer in recent years.

There is general agreement concerning the problem of sterilization, at least as far as the essential aspects are concerned. Any arbitrary destruction or mutilation of human fertility must definitely be denied. Scientific doubts concern those cases only where the health of the entire person calls for an operation. This was generally called, then, "indirect sterilization." There are extreme cases where expert interpretation of the situation clearly arrives at the conclusion that, on the level of natural law—that is to say, a rational evaluation of the facts and of human responsibility—any further fertility must be eliminated for good. An operation performed with these realizations in mind (in order to save a life or a marriage) would, then, in a moral sense, not be a sterilization proper, since it is not a destruction of responsible human fertility; responsible reasoning would exclude it anyhow. Yet these are extreme cases.

One possible solution to the problem of birth control is total abstinence. However, this calls for a tremendous amount of self-control in every respect and it can be beneficial to a marriage only if it works hand in hand with a conscious and careful observance of tender married love.

It is highly important to understand clearly that total abstinence is not a value in itself, especially if its motive is selfishness or coldness. All the methods of birth control are of no avail unless they are accompanied by a genuine spirit of responsibility.

At Corinth, St. Paul had to deal with married people who, in an enthusiasm typical of converts, decided on total abstinence, partly however, because of their expectation of a near second coming of the Lord. The Apostle warns them: "Do not refuse each other except for mutual consent, and then only for an agreed time, to leave yourselves free for prayer; then come together again lest Satan tempt you through lack of self-control" (I Cor. 7:5).

The Council fully realized that it is not so simple to offer total abstinence as *the* solution to all married people. "But where the intimacy of married life is broken off, it is not rare for its faithfulness to be imperiled and its quality of fruitfulness ruined. For then the upbringing of the children and the courage to accept new ones are both endangered" (*Constitution on the Church in the Modern World*, Art. 51).

The least one can surmise from this text is that married people should never refuse each other the expression of marital tenderness, particularly when the circumstances call for a prolonged period of abstinence. Any fear of sexual excitement as a consequence of mutual tenderness must be overcome. Yet, it is absolutely necessary to understand that genuine marital tenderness, as intimate as it might be, has nothing in common with the widespread necking and petting practices of unmarried people. Such petting is rather a mutual sexual exploitation, even though there might be an agreement to go only so far. Marital tenderness is something very special and it is totally different from premarital sex: it is the genuine and respectful expression of togetherness, of mutual loving attention, and vigilance.

As early as 1951, Pope Pius XII already approved of periodical abstinence (rhythm method) as a means of birth regulation, although noted theologians—for example, F. Hurth—thought that it was immoral to consciously choose the infertile days as a means of birth control (Address to the Midwives of Italy). However, Pius XII was very specific about the fact that the motives ought to be the decisive factor. Married people act correctly only if they have sound reasons not to desire any more children at a given time.

Since 1951, periodical abstinence as a method of birth regulation has developed into a highly complicated technique with calendar, body temperature control, observance of abdominal pain, chemical analysis of the vaginal flow and medical counselling. From many pulpits this method was praised as the "Catholic method" and considered as highly safe. Because he spoke more frequently about these issues than about the Paschal mystery and because he hailed this method as being "safe" and dependable, a Cardinal was popularly called the "cardinal-safe-period."

One must not overlook that it was Pius XII who initiated discussions with new aspects on these issues within the Church. His decision left no doubts about the fact that marital intercourse is good and remains so as an expression and furtherance of married love, harmony, and faithfulness, even though the spouses try to sever the intercourse effectively from any possible unwanted pregnancy by means of a calculating method, provided that they have sufficient reasons for doing so. Moreover, the (partly erroneous) praises given to the safety of this method by many bishops, theologians, priests and laymen, made it perfectly clear that a method of birth control is not bad *per se*, just because it is effective.

Yet, it was impossible to avoid the issue: "Why is this method morally good and why are those formerly condemned methods morally bad?" Some gave the following answer: "Because this method does not interfere with the physiological processes of the marital act and its consequences." The argument frequently raised against this position was: "This method is an interference after all, indeed a rather radical interference into the psychological processes which are of higher quality and even more important to man in his entirety than mere physiological processes. Moreover, the objective is the same with reference to the physiological processes, that is, to prevent the union of sperm and egg during an actual marital act." Another answer was: "This method is better than earlier condemned methods, because it does not tamper with the expressiveness and dignity of the marital act." This answer is certainly more convincing than the other that focuses only on the "inviolability of biological processes" but it gives rise to new questions: "What if some recently developed methods do preserve the dignity and integrity of the marital act and are certainly far from having to do with abortion?"

At this point of the discussion, the Council text on marriage and family was worked out. Most important of all, one must see how the question is stated now: harmonization of the needs of conjugal love with the responsible transmission of life.

The first statement of the Council is that the good end does not simply justify the means—an old Catholic principle which is rather topical in comparison with a chaotic situation ethics which even tries to approve everything including abortion (*e.g.*, Joseph Fletcher, *Situation Ethics*). In addition, the Council offers positive criteria: "Therefore when there is question of harmonizing conjugal love with the responsible transmission of life, the moral aspect of any procedure does not depend solely on sincere intentions or on an evaluation of motives. It must be determined by objective standards. These, based on the nature of the human person and his acts, preserve the full sense of mutual self-giving and human procreation in the context of true love" (*Constitution on the Church in the Modern World*, Art. 51). Upon the wish of Pope Paul, it was pointed out: "Such a goal cannot be achieved unless the virtue of conjugal chastity is sincerely practiced." This is of great importance. It must be clearly understood that the development of the doctrines of the Church and the answers to new questions cannot be a matter of watering down Christian morality. The criteria listed by the Council demand of every spouse a constant vigilance with regard to the true nature of the marital act, mutual respect and frequently the mortification of selfish tendencies.

Yet it cannot be overlooked that the Council did not even touch on that criterion which seemed to be the only decisive one according to a traditionalist conception, that is, the absolute inviolability of physiological processes which would have to characterize every single marital act as a potential act of procreation. Certainly, the Council Fathers would not have omitted to emphasize this criterion if it had been an unquestionable criterion in their eyes (in their entirety or majority).

The famous footnote 14 which makes reference to the rather strict formulations of *Casti connubii*, cannot simply be interpreted as an affirmation and re-emphasis of these formulations given forty years ago, since the same footnote also mentions the comparatively revolutionary address of Pope Pius XII and an address delivered by Pope Paul VI on June 23, 1964, which announced the existence of a papal commission for the study of the issues involved, yet warning against too hasty hopes with reference to a change in the directives of the Church. It goes without saying that neither laymen nor theologians will have the final say in these matters: it will be up to the Pope alone. Popes have had the final say about the permissibility of moderate usury, about the non-existence of a direct power of the Church in temporal and political matters, about the immorality of witch hunts and torture. Thereby they corrected fallible announcements of preceding popes who, because of a different historical context did neither see nor discern clearly. But the entire people of God somehow were instrumental in the final clarification through prayer, study or experience. Individual theologians decisively initiated the useful and necessary distinctions. At the end of a period of development it was always clear that the moral values stated in previous documents of the Church, were not only preserved, but even better, clarified through finer distinctions and sometimes corrections.

The decisive values relative to marital chastity which were mainly protected by the past tradition of the Church and which must always be protected, appear to me to be the following:

1) It is a blessing for a man to be born; procreation is basically good.

2) The transmission of life and upbringing in the family must be envisioned in their entirety and interdependence. It is not good to procreate unless there is the will and the possibility to educate the child properly.

3) The marital act and its dignity are of high moral significance.

4) The life of a child is inviolable beginning with the moment of conception.

Under the still controversial assumption that not every interference with the physiological realm is immoral, the following tentative guidelines for a solution might be considered: If an act of birth regulation is in the interest of the person (of the spouses as persons and of their genuine interpersonal relationship) and if it is necessary, then that action must be preferred which, all things considered, is the most dignified and which preserves the total meaning of the marital act best. Points for consideration include marital faithfulness, the continuation of the marriage, the atmosphere of harmony and love which is so necessary for the education of children, the readiness of desire for further children at the proper time. Thereby, the differences in personality and cultural background must be given due consideration. Moral solutions which can only be offered to privileged strata and nations are suspect in view of the Gospel. A moral theologian must always have the under-privileged and the poor in mind, for the salvation, the gradual progress and dignity of *every* human being is at stake!

What I said represents merely an attempt which, to be sure, is gaining wider and wider recognition. Many questions are yet left open. The entire people of God, above all those who possess special knowledge, experience, and intuition, must continue to investigate how, under given conditions, the full meaning of marital devotion and the readiness to joyfully fulfill the marital calling can be pre-served and furthered. Once again, it must be clearly under-stood that the final word is up to the teaching authority in the Church whenever fundamental moral aspects are involved. Reverence for the majesty of truth that must be sought carefully and inflinchingly, and for the authority of the successor of Peter and the bishops of the world, bind us in duty to remain patient. Doctrinal solutions cannot be achieved overnight, nor is it possible to bury vital issues. Questions which are not yet ripe should be left open.

If we all clearly realize the abundance of lasting values and principles, if we develop and cultivate them in full vigilance and if we regard the controversies with Christian prudence, vigilance, humility and patience, then the present discussions cannot do us any harm; rather, they become a call to thoroughness, to a more mature and at the same time more demanding and understanding morality.

CHAPTER FOURTEEN

Family Relationships

Although God's commandment: "Honor your father and your mother" (Ex 20:12) is addressed to men of all times and places, the fulfillment of this charge is greatly conditioned by man's historical setting. It is the task of both speculative and applied ethics to present principles of moral conduct within the general framework of lasting values. Today we are fully aware of the far-reaching influence which the "father image" exerts on both the conscious and unconscious levels of man's religious conscience. The full realization of this truth urges us to rid ourselves of an obsolete and distorted father image in both morality and religion.

It would be beyond the competence of empirical psychology to infer from Freud's psychoanalytical experiences that the son invariably develops a kind of Oedipus complex and that a secret rebellion against his father gives impetus to his psychological energies. On the other hand, it cannot be denied that very early in life dangerous conflicts, not only against one's earthly father but against all authority figures including that of the heavenly Father, may develop in the deepest recesses of the child's psychological experiences.

In a similar manner, early childhood experiences with a tyrannical and overly strict father are the roots of irrational and disproportionate guilt complexes. Deep-seated rebellion against a feudalistic or paternalistic "father image" of the Church often goes hand in hand with an overt rebellion against any despotic or outdated exercise of parental authority. One of the principal sources for social tensions, for distorted personalities, and for unbelief and rebellion against the Church, arises from the stubborn adherence to old-fashioned regimes in the exercise of authority in the family, in the Church, and in society at large. The paternalistic "ruler" or "prince of the Church" patterned after the despotic age of his forefathers, who in all matters poses as the infallible representative of God, becomes an insurmountable obstacle to man's search for God.

Family Life—a Partnership

In primitive society, woman played a significant role in providing sustenance to the family through the tilling of the soil in gardens and fields. A husband left father and mother to follow his wife and her maternal clan. However, with the introduction of domesticated animals and improved methods of agriculture, man emerged as the undisputed manager of a predominantly paternal family. The book of Genesis considers the dominion of man over woman the result of original sin and, at the same time, symbolic of man's need for redemption (Cf Gen 3:17). We see this wrong attitude in the worst form when Lamech, the descendant of Cain, married two women and tyrannized them (Cf 4:19-24). Man, after gaining superiority over woman, also invented the double standard in morality. This is seen in the ancient law where the unfaithful woman was condemned to die, while the equally guilty man was left to go unpunished.

The position of woman was favorably influenced by the religious ideas expressed in God's covenant with His chosen people—a covenant which takes its imagery from the love relationship between husband and wife. In the light of the sacramental dignity of marriage, the redeemed husband is called to a humble love similar to that of our Lord for His Church. Thereby man becomes liberated and redeemed from his selfish desire to rule over his wife. Thus religion attacked the faulty and debasing structures of ancient family life even before the time of full social reform. The Gospel teaches a new attitude to women, although the New Testament is still abounding in many admonitions regarding obedience and subjection for women. This was in keeping with the prevailing conditions of family life and social institutions of that time. In our modern civilization, family life has become a system of partnership. Husband and wife mutually listen and express their opinions so that decisions by consent can be achieved. They mutually relinquish selfish desires where a compromise is needed. Mere autocratic ruling, on the part of the husband as the lord of the house, undermines his true moral authority.

The times are gone when a girl is given in marriage by her father. Today the choice of marriage partners is a mutual one between two young people. Their relationship is characterized by reciprocal respect and devotion so essential to a community of perfect partnership.

In our desire for an ultimate resolution of social and religious tensions in today's society, we should concentrate our efforts toward a fuller implementation of the partnership idea to all realms of life. There is no doubt that priests and bishops, raised in families where interpersonal relationships were characterized by the idea of partnership, will have a different approach to the exercise of their authority when compared with members of the clergy coming from autocratic and paternalistic families where the wife and children were kept in the role of servants and where the son impatiently waited for the day of emancipation when he could rule his own family.

The whole pattern of today's democratic style of living largely determines the mutual relationships between parents and children. Children should be helped to mature gradually to share in family partnership and social responsibility. In past ages where young people even after their marriage remained within the patriarchal structure, the raising of children primarily aimed at obedience and loyalty to the clan. Today such practices would have serious consequences for both the individual and society. Today our aim must be the education of children toward an ever more mature sharing of responsibility.

Authority and Obedience

Past approaches to obedience in both teaching and practice were extremely one-sided. They failed to stress the truly Christian meaning of authority and its genuine exercise. Guides for the examination of conscience abounded in categories of sins for those ruled, while no matter for the examination of conscience was included for rulers such as Church dignitaries (popes and bishops), religious superiors, or worldly dignitaries and executives. How could a person rendering such passive and unenlightened obedience ever be expected to mature into the role of the superior and effectively discharge his duties?

God's authority is primarily one of love, based on the inscrutable decrees of divine wisdom to call creatures into being in order to make them the concelebrants of His own divine love. Freedom in our relationship to God connotes a grateful acceptance of His dominion and authority. It is important to note that God does not demand an obedience of slaves. He made us His free sons and daughters. God preferred to create man free even at the risk of a possible misuse of that freedom, rather than to subject him to blind and slavish obedience. Through his own selfish disobedience, man jeopardized the integrity of his God-given freedom. On the other hand, Christ's redemption calls man to a freedom of loving obedience. By a mutual and all-embracing love, we participate in God's freedom as His sons and daughters. As children of God, we are given the basic guidelines for this freedom. Christ solemnly announced: "This is my commandment: love one another, as I have loved you. . . . I shall not call you servants any more, because a servant does not know his master's business; I call you friends, because I have made known to you everything I have learnt from my Father" (Jn 15:12-15).

God the Father is the eternal source of Christ's magnitude of love and filial freedom. The Son's own love for us is designed to lead us to the Father, the source of all authority. His love is life-giving and authoritative. Christ's commandment of love extends beyond the mere "Thou shalt"; it embraces the motivation, the power and the authority of love: "As the Father has loved me, so I have loved you. Remain in my love" (Jn 15:9). Ultimately, the commandment of love receives its meaning and its liberating and binding force only in view of Christ's love. His love invites us to reciprocate His charity in an all-embracing exercise of love. The very authority of Christ is rooted in His love. The fulfillment of Christ's new commandment becomes easy if we unite ourselves with His charity. Thus obedience becomes personal fulfillment in an increasing freedom.

Parental authority, in analogy to the Creator's and Redeemer's love, must be a life-giving love. It has its roots in the conjugal love which makes parents accept and desire children so that they might become the concelebrants of their own love. If parents fail to accept the child as a person in a genuine and wholehearted love, their authority becomes void of true authenticity. Their God-ordained authority becomes even more marred if they arbitrarily enforce their authority in order to "break their children's will" instead of guiding them to a free and responsible type of obedience which is based on understanding and insight.

Today, more than ever before, parental authority should provide an atmosphere conducive to individual initiative and freedom. Therefore, parents should refrain from literally smothering their children with commands and restrictions in so many do's and don'ts. They should not surround the adolescent with excessive regulations. In other words, they ought to help their children toward greater independence even at the risk of errors and mistakes. We certainly should not provide a favorable environment for errors and blunders. Yet all of us, whether we want it or not, will make a certain number of mistakes. Similar to learning a new language, we are unable to learn it unless we take the risk of learning it through trials and errors. On the other hand, the courage to make mistakes without the initiative to learn from our experience is likewise doomed to failure. Young people need encouragement and a fair amount of freedom of action with fair amount of supervision.

Today some of the Church's critics are rather arrogant. Proposals for reform and critical judgments are presented in a tone of certain infallibility. This syndrome, on the whole, can be compared with the stage of development in puberty when the human being, on awakening to a fuller self-consciousness, will act with an air of increasing infallibility as he perceives the established order of society and the bearers of authority impose their commands and opinions as infallible laws. An autocratic manner of imposing authority in the family and the Church tends to undermine the very roots of the established order. This is probably due to both a subconscious and unconscious process in man. If, on the other hand, parents would present their opinions with modesty and simplicity, admitting their own mistakes, there would be less arrogance in adolescents. Just as filial arrogance is found with "infallible" parents, so likewise in the Church we find the most severe criticism and tensions in the dioceses and provinces of "infallible" bishops and superiors. Modesty in the exercise of authority is more likely to produce sincere obedience than the constant pounding on one's authority.

Those who expect the pope to make clear declarations of infallibility or clear-cut statements in matters pertaining to natural law, that is to say in issues not involving divine revelation, have failed to recognize the true functions of authority as taught by social psychology. Similarly misled are those who fail to take the pronouncements of the pope or the Council seriously, unless these are spoken in terms of infallibility. A rather authoritarian type of archbishop, quite vocal in his criticism of Pope John and the Ecumenical Council, when questioned as to his allegiance and obedience to the Church, responded that the Council has not spoken with infallibility and consequently cannot oblige him to allegiance and obedience. It is hoped that the so-called "liberals" in the Church will not subscribe to such a kind of "selective disobedience" which is found in the authoritarian reactionaries. Humble obedience is possible only where a truly humble exercise of authority is found. Such humble obedience will never be blind but rather enlightened in regard to the innate limitations of one's own judgments. This requires an enlightened acceptance of unavoidable limitations in the one commanding, as well as a permissive

F

attitude of those in authority, such as parents and Church leaders, so that children and the faithful at large can exercise a certain amount of spontaneity. Similarly, children have to be permissive with their parents and their limitations. A sense of humor is a wonderful asset to the Christian, especially if the bishops, or even the pope, should act or speak in ways less perfect than expected.

The Dialogue Between the Generations

Any crisis of authority and obedience is usually associated with the problems between the older and younger generations. This problem is more exaggerated today because various age groups subscribe to different outlooks on life. Young people speak an entirely different language although they may have some concepts in common with the older generation. The style of life for the younger generation greatly differs from that of the middle-aged and senior citizens. Youth is critical of both institutions and customs when such appear phony, formalistic and empty. The younger generation's protest against obsolete laws and regulations should not be considered as rebellion against authority or the established order and morality.

In reality, the qualities of the different generations should be complimentary and therefore a potential positive factor. The resulting tension between the different age groups may stimulate progress in continuity, and likewise continuity in progress. Tensions may become truly fruitful, in a Christian sense, if they are approached and resolved in the spirit of love, patience and mutual respect.

The fundamental law for the dialogue between the generations is that of mutual listening so that issues, which unite as well as separate us, can be properly evaluated. We may find a common background, a common concern, or a common heritage, even in regard to points of disagreement. In addition to a sincere dialogue, we need a humble realization of a constantly expanding knowledge which can rectify and modify our own opinions.

In past ages, adolescents were expected to mature peacefully while adapting themselves to the traditional forms and customs of life. In the event of difficulties, it was invariably presumed that the organization or institution embodied the greater wisdom. It was an accepted truth that only youth needed to learn something. Granted that in this dynamic society the wisdom of the experienced and at the same time openminded mature person is able to make a significant contribution, we should also recognize the special qualities which characterize the young, such as enthusiasm, initiative and a keen desire for a radical and genuine sincerity.

Our age demands of both young and old a mentality which not only tolerates differences of opinions, but tries to weigh and appreciate their positive values. In certain areas of mutual concern, united and immediate action with a fair compromise would be the best course of action. Even if young people are unable to share the appreciation for certain pious exercises or moral convictions of the older generation, they still should accept and respect these as meaningful expressions of their elders. Reciprocally, it would be well for adults to tolerate and respect the attitudes of the rising generation. I would like to illustrate the above by a personal experience: Last year when celebrating Holy Mass in the Cathedral at Cuernavaca, Mexico, my German mentality was first displeased with the type of liturgical music and singing since it was genuinely Mexican and ultramodern. However, I immediately noticed that all this was very meaningful to the people and it seemed close to their real life. Therefore, I soon was completely taken over by their passionate display of faith which all of a sudden had become meaningful and significant even to me, a stranger.

Mutual Responsibility for Salvation

Christ endowed His Church with a definite pastoral character. This presupposes respective attitudes and a decidedly pastoral approach in all those charged with special responsibilities for the salvation of other members of the community. This, however, does not minimize or exclude the mutual pastoral concern and responsibility which is the duty of all Christians. At times, some members of the Christian community, endowed with special charisms and not burdened by offices and obligations, are in a better position to work for the salvation of their brethren than even the consecrated priest.

The same truth applies to pastoral concerns for one's family members. The spouses are basically responsible for each other's salvation as mutual shepherds of their souls. In addition, parents are the "first preachers of the faith to their children" (*Constitution on the Church,* Art. 11). It is their noble task to convey to their children the gladsome tidings of the Gospel and of the Christian life which was transmitted to them in Baptism. The parent's sincere respect for the personal dignity of each child, together with their sincere love and firm discipline, not only gives testimony of their own faith but confirms the faith in their children's hearts. Their example provides the child with firsthand experience of the nobility of a truly Christian life. Parents fulfill their priestly task when they make their family a community worshiping God in true faith, hope and confident love. We should never expect children to accept the message of the Gospel slavishly. Mutual acceptance in family living implies cooperation and collaboration in the "give and take" of daily life.

The *Pastoral Constitution on the Church in the Modern World* throws special light on the reciprocal character of man's responsibility in relation to authority. "Thus the family is a foundation of society. In it the various generations come together and help one another to grow wiser and to harmonize personal rights with the other requirements of social life" (*Pastoral Constitution on the Church in the Modern World*, Art. 52). It would be for the greatest benefit of our society if every member in the family were to recognize and accept his special role in behalf of the whole. Authority is at its best when it provides an atmosphere conducive to the full personality development through a reciprocal sharing of responsibility.

Parents are endowed with a special type of authority. Nevertheless, they reach their fulfillment only through a loving dependence on God's own authority. Docility and gratitude to God tend to make parents open-minded and grateful to their own children. The Council states: "As living members of the family, children contribute in their own way to making their parents holy" (*Pastoral Constitution on the Church in the Modern World*, Art. 48). Children have a decided responsibility for the salvation of their parents which they can best meet within the realm of genuine love and gratitude.

CHAPTER FIFTEEN

Celibacy for the Sake
of the Kingdom of Heaven

In many civilizations single life and childlessness have been considered a particularly harsh fate if not a punishment from God. Christ spoke (Cf Mt 19:12) of those who are incapable of marriage, "born so from their mother's womb" or "made so by man," whose continence means privation, suffering, and perhaps injustice. But distinct from them, he spoke also of the continence that is a free personal choice "for the sake of the Kingdom of heaven." "Let him accept it who can," He said.

Accordingly, there has been in Christ's church a continuing history of this voluntarily dedicated continence that is a gift of grace and a testimony to the blessedness of the Kingdom of heaven. To appreciate the true nature of this continence, we must distinguish its essential and lasting message of salvation from conditions that result from the necessities and circumstances of an era.

Testimony to the Coming of the Kingdom of God

The synoptics describe Jesus' sermon as the message of the Kingdom of God that comes with Him and through Him. God takes possession of the human heart. The manifestation of His love guide men and deliver them from an enslaving attachment to temporal things. The Kingdom of God, the Kingdom of heaven, is infinitely more than all the powers and forces of this world and this age. It extends beyond all earthly experience. Christ Himself does not

derive His human nature and His mission here on earth
from "flesh and blood," not from that most powerful of
earthly forces, the union of man and woman. Neither does
Christ, who is the final and perfect man, build His house
and family on an earthly foundation. Those who have
been chosen by Him to be the sons and daughters of God
must recognize that they do not owe this privilege "to
the urge of the flesh and the will of man" (Cf Jn 1:12).
The Kingdom of heaven is not merely the open future of
a happy family and a better constituted society; it is a
direct and immediate openness in life eternal.

The presence of the Kingdom of heaven is perfectly
shown in Christ Himself, in a life that goes beyond all
that man has ever experienced or yearned for. Since the
fullness of the Spirit rests with Him and He lives wholly
for the Father, He does not think of Himself. He is not
concerned to preserve His life. The splendor and power
of earthly kingdoms is not for Him; nor does He choose
the way of marriage, although He is more capable of love
than any man ever was. His total commitment is to the
will and the love of the Father and to an unconditional
dedication to all men. The testimony of His celibacy must
be seen in this totality through His sermons, in the testimony of his life, in the signs of the dominion of God and,
above all, in the Easter mystery of death and resurrection.

There is no law imposed on the disciples of Christ to
leave everything—father, mother, house, and wife—in order
to follow Him in total dedication to the Kingdom of heaven;
it is their own free and joyous decision. Made today, this
decision reflects the characteristics of the new era, of the
new freedom and the new hope. The disciple who knows
he is only on pilgrimage here on this earth is already filled
with the beatitudes. His heart yearns for only one thing:
to please the Lord (Cf I Cor 4:32), to concentrate all his

energies on the propagation of the Good
dedicate himself to the service of brotherly

This enthusiastic self-liberation for the sake
Lord and His gospel is ultimately rooted, not in expectation
of His *parousia* in a near future, but in the realization that
the Lord and His dominion of love are already at hand. It
is not the "shortness of time" that creates the urgency but
the compressed and pressing fullness of this time of salvation
in which the final coming of the Lord is prepared. The
usual translation of I Cor 7:29 as "the time is growing
short" is open to criticism. Physical time would have to
be rendered in Greek as *"chronos,"* whereas *"kairos"* is
the hour of salvation, charged with divine energies. This
is not only short for every man—for instance in comparison
with eternal destiny—but "compressed," "fulfilled and
pressing" (*synestalménos*). That is why this unique hour
of salvation addresses both married and unmarried in the
form of a gift and a call to radical freedom for the cause of
the Lord.

Voluntary celibacy has special value as testimony to
the urgency of the *kairos*. It is a charism, a blessed enthu-
siam for the Good News of the dominion of God, a free
and fervent dedication to His gospel and the service thereof;
it is total surrender to Christ and the coming of His
kingdom.

In my opinion it would be wrong to say simply that
voluntary continence for the sake of the Kingdom of heaven
makes the person who chooses this life a better disciple of
Christ than the one who marries. But since marriage precedes the coming of the Kingdom of God as a natural
choice of life, all those capable of marriage would ordinar-
ly marry regardless of the impending dominion of God.
Hence celibacy, freely chosen and joyfully experienced, is
a particularly eloquent testimony to the blessedness of the

gospel and to the liberating and urgent impact of the coming of the Kingdom.

The definition of the Council of Trent, according to which it must be denied "that it is better and more blessed to remain single than to marry" (Session XXIV Canon 1, *Denzinger* No. 1910) must be interpreted, in my opinion, with the emphasis on "more blessed" (*beatius*). This "more blessed" cannot be grasped within the categories of a humanistic morality of self-perfection. Its meaning becomes wholly distorted in any context of earned spiritual status. Rather, this is God's own gift of a blessedness that pours out the Good News of the approaching Kingdom of heaven, it is a special gift of the Holy Spirit: the blessedness of a charism in the service of the gospel, or a witness for the Kingdom.

Martyrdom and Celibacy

The celibacy of Christ must be seen in the light of His testimony (*martyrion*) in the Easter mystery. The announcement of the Kingdom of God was most intimately connected with martyrdom during the days of the infant Church. The martyr witnessed in a unique way the power of faith as well as the Good News of the eternal kingdom whose reality could be already felt here and now. Since the days of the Apostles, a similar testimonial value has been attributed to consecrated celibacy, truly lived.

In the Constantinian era, when martyrdom had become a rarity and when many members of the official Church had established themselves in the earthly splendor of an imperial Church, and the descendants of the Apostles became princes of the Empire and "princes of the Church," the testimony of those who, in full freedom, chose poverty and a single life as their lot, assumed special value as a loving yet firm protest against the secularization of the Church. The testimony of monks and virgins withstood the tension between the eschatologically understood Kingdom of God and the "princedom" of many a churchman and ecclesiastical institution, and did so without lapsing into rebellion against authority. The fact that popes and bishops, who themselves were enamored of the splendor, pagentry, power, and privileges of a Church that leaned more and more toward worldliness, nevertheless approved of the testimony of the celibate, must not be underestimated from a religious point of view.

The celibacy of an ever increasing number of monks in the East and in the West, of the bishops of the East and the entire clergy in the West, helped substantially in saving the Church from total corruption and the feudalism of powerful families. If at times the Apostolic See and bishoprics became bones of contention and the sport of powerful families that fought over benefices, prebends and fiefs, despite the still existing celibacy of the priests, how much worse the situation would have been if the ideal of celibacy had vanished entirely! The scandalous behavior of an Alexander VI who, though unmarried, could not care less about celibacy, and who appointed his son, the robber-chief Cesare Borgia, to be a cardinal, amply testifies to this danger.

To be sure, the Church benefitted only to the extent that celibacy was really understood and embraced because of its intrinsic value. This will always be so, for it must ever be clearly seen that the law of celibacy, understood chiefly as a law or, even worse, misunderstood as a necessity for the freedom of the Church in a purely sociological sense, becomes valueless and absurd. Only its essential motivation measures the dimension of its testimony to the Kingdom of heaven.

Social Recognition of Those Who Are Single

In the epoch of the family-group, when two or three generations lived under the same roof, an unmarried person had his place in this group and thus enjoyed social recognition and incorporation. The number of single people was relatively high during some periods in the past because the scope and number of family enterprises could not be increased at will in an agricultural society that had, to a considerable degree, already reached its saturation point. Those members of a family who remained single were usually welcomed and appreciated on the parental farm or in the parental workshop.

This social structure largely favored the spread of religious community life. One need only remember Ireland. During the past generations a large part of the population saw clearly that, unless they emigrated, they could never have families of their own. When the parental farm was small, it was simply not advisable to remain within one's own family. To choose the priesthood or life in a convent meant in any case social incorporation into a community whose model remained the family-group. Frequently it meant definite social advancement as well.

Beginning with the dawn of industrialization, the picture has changed fundamentally. As far as the economics of the situation is concerned, everyone who has learned a trade, indeed everyone who is healthy and willing to work, can now marry and have a family of his own. In our modern society the right to marry is considered one of the most fundamental of human rights. But single people and those who do not belong to a religious family are not at all in the same position as their brothers and sisters of older days. Often they live alone and in many cases they do not possess full social and family status. They are confronted in their society with an anonymous, or a least a largely de-humanized, labor world on one hand, and on the other—as a sort of counterbalance—a world where the intimate life of marriage and family is valued more highly than ever.

Particularly difficult is the situation of men and women who have been left by their spouses or who are divorced. Those who never married have generally formed substantial lasting friendships within a social group, but these others are often totally alone and feel quite painfully the anomaly of their position. There is little doubt that the fate of the single person today, regardless of the cause of their single status, presents more psychological and sociological problems than in those days when an unmarried person was fully incorporated into a stable family in a relatively static community.

In this new situation the testimony of celibacy, freely and joyfully chosen for the sake of the Kingdom of heaven, is newly accented and of particular value, provided that it is not lived in an atmosphere of isolation from family and society. Many people who are deprived of marriage due to human factors can find support and orientation through the One who gave up marriage of His own free will. The testimony of those who follow Christ in celibacy can somehow discover for them, in a situation seemingly forced upon them, more possibilities for fulfillment in loving service than they could have thought possible. It can unfold for them their own personal *kairos*, and reveal how they can "use to the full this present time of salvation" (Eph 5:8).

Celibacy for the sake of the Kingdom contains within itself the power to build a community of salvation. The Kingdom of heaven is the gathering call of divine love. When it will be fully revealed there will be a perfect community of blessed love. The way to that perfection is through the expression of shared friendship with Christ in the community of His disciples.

Retreat into the desert, the life of a hermit, may be a stage in the life of one who remains single for the sake of the Kingdom of heaven, but it cannot be *the* final and classical realization of his vocation. Celibacy does, indeed, free from a constricting membership in a clan or family insofar as the family is a purely worldly and social group. But one of the most precious fruits of religious celibacy is that cordial and strong fraternal love that establishes a new family, a family that, together with the Christian family but in its own way, reflects the blessed community of the saints and manifests the gathering power of the Kingdom of God.

Today it must be understood more clearly than ever that free abstention from marriage does not mean the total renunciation of any family-type community. On the contrary, its task is to construct the most stable form of community and friendship, the community of disciples gathered around the Master. Those who remain single for the sake of the Kingdom of heaven can thus offer to a world, whose depersonalized character demands the counterbalance of a truly personal community, the welcome message that one who is unmarried is not condemned to isolation. Due to his particular situation he is called upon to work in a community founded entirely on faith and the love of Christ.

The celibate priest ought not to be only a friend, brother and father to all those who need him. Even to achieve this goal he, too, needs the cordial friendship and community of his brothers. Less than ever before can monasteries be mere communities of workers with their own special rules, discipline, and administration. They must not be perturbed by a pathological fear of false friendships or of close contact with their fellowmen. Rather, they should embody in those communities of disciples to which they belong, that cordial friendship for one another—and for all men—that testifies to the presence of the Divine Master.

On the basis of this very realization we should be especially thoughtful of the involuntarily unmarried and the deserted spouses and widows. It is particularly these who stand in dire need of cordial friendship and social recognition. The founding of a congregation for widows and deserted women is one of the most daring attempts to contribute to the solution of this problem. Much more needs to be done. The attention of our parishes, of the relatives and friends of these single people, of secular institutions and of religious people are all required to find answers to this problem. The testimony of happy and fruitful continence, which is in itself valuable, and the concrete realization of a community formed on this basis should, indeed, coincide with the concern and the many initiatives now developing in behalf of those leading a single life.

Celibacy in View of Today's Spirituality of Marriage

Religiously based celibacy has new aspects not only in view of the new structure of the family and the new, often painful, position of those leading a single life, but also in relation to today's new spirituality of marriage.

In the past, the family-group could develop into a power that impeded the joyful acceptance of the Kingdom of heaven, or else, redeemed of its complacency, it could develop into an ideal embodiment of the community of salvation. It was part of the mission and testimony of those vowed to celibacy to prepare the way to this redeemed self-understanding.

Today, in an administrated and practically organized world, the intimate personal community between husband and wife and the immediate family has assumed a new significance. In this we sense the danger of concentrating all hopes on marriage as such, and of thus exposing more than ever to frustration, spiritual isolation, and despondency, those who must do without marriage. Under these circumstances celibacy for the sake of the Kingdom of heaven also takes on a new significance in that—provided it is a convincing testimony of real freedom and true fulfillment—it liberates from unredeemed ties of "flesh and blood" while it binds one to his fellowman in loving communion through ties of the spirit.

If we find—as we do—that our present time is marked by an almost primitive worship of sexual fulfillment, as if it possessed redeeming power in itself, we also find that a deeper understanding of marriage as a vocation and as a way to sainthood has evolved. We may attribute this development in some degree to the testimony of celibacy understood in the truly Christian sense. But this new understanding of marriage is by no means a mere modification of monastic spirituality; it is a development in its own right, wherein Christian families strive for sainthood and testify to the presence of divine love.

The understanding of the unmarried state for the sake of the Kingdom of God can profit from today's spirituality of marriage. The young people of today understand much more clearly than a few generations ago that the choice of a celibate life is religiously absurd if it is not accompanied, indeed preceded, by a high esteem for marriage and a proper understanding of the Christian vocation of marriage. Knowing how good marriage is, celibacy can never be misinterpreted as abstention from "sour grapes," but must be seen for what it really is: love-in-action, the whole-hearted presentation to God of the first fruits of the earth and all the energies of love.

Well educated Christian spouses now know, from the unfolding teachings of the Church, that their fertility for the Kingdom of heaven is in proportion to the genuine conjugal love that forms the root and the shape of their parental responsibility and love. Faced with this example, the unmarried will see more clearly than ever that the value of their testimony and the spiritual fruitfulness of their celibacy are decisively determined by the strength of their truly personal communion and by their cordial fraternal and paternal (or maternal) love for all the children of God.

CHAPTER SIXTEEN

Conversion to Ecumenical Thinking and Acting

"The Lord and Ages wisely and patiently follows out the plan of His grace on behalf of us sinners. In recent times He has begun to bestow more generously upon divided Christians remorse over their divisions and a longing for unity. Everywhere, large numbers have felt the impulse of this grace...." With these words, the *Decree on Ecumenism* (Art. 1) traces the ecumenical movement and its progress. It shows the Catholic Church sincerely repentant for past failures, as indicated by "a remarkable admission of guilt" and humble trust in God's mercy and grace. The decree describes "sincere remorse" as a special grace.

There is no doubt that the Church's active participation in the ecumenical movement must begin with the "Confiteor" in which we acknowledge our own fault instead of a self-righteous pointing to our separated brethren and their ecclesial communities. The more faithfully we respond to God's grace by a humble admission of our shortcomings and a courageous effort to rectify our errors, the more we can rely on the assistance of God's grace to enlighten other Christian communities to make their own admission of guilt.

Contrite Commitment to the Great Commandment

Love and unity are our Lord's great commandment and final legacy. "The Church by her relationship with Christ is a kind of sacrament or sign of intimate union with God and of the unity of all mankind" (*Constitution on the Church*, Art. 1). In view of the mystery of Christ's passion, death and resurrection, our Lord prays for His Apostles and all those who accepted the faith in consequence of their sermons and genuine testimony of unity: "I have given them the glory you gave to me, that they may be one as we are one. With me in them and you in me, may they be so completely one that the world will realize that it was you who sent me and that I have loved them as much as you loved me" (Jn 17:22-23).

In order to reconcile man with God and, at the same time, with his fellowmen, Jesus not only submitted Himself to the baptism of repentance at the banks of the Jordan, but likewise to the bloody baptism on the Cross. The act of atonement opens the way to unity. Christ carries on His shoulders the heavy burden of mankind's sinful past. In Christ's sacrifice of atonement we recognize the law of salvation: Guilt and sin must first be atoned before healing and a wholesome future may be expected. This truth finds special application to the ecumenical movement which is meant to lead Christians from strife and discord to full unity and an all-embracing charity.

The Council has made a remarkable admission of past errors and guilt on the part of the Catholic Church and its official representatives, not only in the *Decree on Ecumenism*, but also in the two conciliatory rites; namely, the interfaith prayer service of the Pope with the observers to the Council in the Basilica of St. Paul, and in the contrite retraction of previous declarations of excommunication between Rome and Constantinople. However, the value of such expressions of contrition remain questionable if, due to the remoteness of past failures, they leave us completely untouched and unconcerned.

There is a hypocritical way of throwing stones at Innocence III, Boniface VIII, Leo X, and Alexander VI, while we feel comfortable in the ivory tower of our self-righteousness. Yet it makes excellent sense to ask forgiveness of our Christian brethren for all our faults and arrogance in defending these mistakes. Up until now we have not only rationalized these blunders but even continued to make them in one way or another. The Second Vatican Council does not permit an easy retreat into the past when the admission of guilt is concerned. It rather demands that, after a sincere examination of conscience, we contritely face our age, tainted with past and present burdens which have not been fully accepted and repaired. "Their primary duty is to make an honest and careful appraisal of whatever needs to be renewed and achieved in the Catholic household itself, in order that its life may bear witness more loyally and luminously to the teachings and ordinances which have been handed down from Christ through the Apostles" (*Decree on Ecumenism*, Art 4). It is important to remember that popes, bishops and religious superiors are included in the body of the faithful. They are not standing aloft on a mighty baroque pulpit in order to castigate the faithful as the "others."

On the other hand, by "faithful" we understand all those who have faith. Consequently, when speaking of remorse, conversion and reform, we do not simply admit the faults of prelates. We all strike our own breasts as we humbly say: "My own fault." The appeal to repentance is addressed not only to the individuals, but also to the whole community of Christians. The Church, as a basic prerequisite to full conversion, must subject all its institutions, its liturgy, canon law, its administrative practices, its interpersonal relationships and its financial transactions, to a thorough and humble examination of conscience. In this respect, the *Decree on Ecumenism* is very clear and emphatic.

This new approach may shock those who hitherto have believed that their love and devotion to the Church obliged them to defend all actions of the Church and its institutions. "Every renewal of the Church essentially consists in an increase of fidelity to her own calling. Undoubtedly, this explains the dynamism of the movement toward unity. Christ summons the Church, as she goes her pilgrim way, to that continual reformation of which she always has need, insofar as she is an institution of men here on earth. Therefore, if the influence of events or of the times has led to deficiencies in conduct, in Church discipline, or even in the formulation of doctrine (which must be carefully distinguished from the deposit of faith itself), these should be appropriately rectified at the proper moment" (*Decree on Ecumenism*, Art. 6).

Consequently, in her acceptance of the ecumenical movement among Christianity, the Catholic Church commits herself to a soul-searching examination of conscience. The Church's institutions and practices must be measured against the criterion of the great commandment of love and the prayer of our Lord "that they all may be one." This prayer for unity also embraces that part of Christianity which is still separated from the See of Peter. In this regard the Council states: "There can be no ecumenism worthy of the name without a change of heart" (*Decree on Ecumenism*, Art. 7).

Ecumenism as Expression of the Worship of God

A one-sided apologetic view which only recognizes light on one's own side of the fence, while it seeks indisputable night and darkness on the other side, is not merely an insurmountable obstacle to Christian unity. It is, above all, a sin against due worship of God. Self-righteousness tends to blind us to the wonderful works of God's grace in other Christian communities. Our failure to admit God's action in their behalf borders on blasphemy. The recognition and acknowledgment of all the good on the other side must lead us further than mere formal dialogue. Our ecumenical efforts become genuine, sincere, credible, and convincing only when we acknowledge their genuine witness to Christ.

The *Decree on Ecumenism* duly emphasizes this aspect: "Catholics must joyfully acknowledge and esteem the truly Christian endowments from our common heritage which are to be found among our separated brethren. It is right and salutary to recognize the riches of Christ and virtuous works in the lives of others who are bearing witness to Christ, sometimes even to the shedding of their blood. For God is always wonderful in His works and worthy of admiration. Nor should we forget that whatever is wrought by the grace of the Holy Spirit in the hearts of our sep- arated brethren can contribute to our own edification" (*Decree on Ecumenism*, Art. 4). The reader will certainly not overlook the style and tone of the preface. This ap- proach to the worship of God, and the acknowledgment of the workings of God in the separated or not yet fully returned Churches and ecclesial communities and their members, will make possible the much desired co-celebra- tion of the Eucharist as a decisive sign of unity.

Basic Rules for the Ecumenical Dialogue

The ecumenical dialogue is based on the spirit of sincere contrition and genuine desire for true worship of God. Such an attitude will enable us to overcome our historical burden and undue feelings of guilt and self-righteousness. The way to unity will then lead us along the ecumenical dialogue—still to be learned and along the path of united action in the service of the entire human family. The basic rules for the ecumenical dialogue may well be summarized as follows:

1. *Our foremost duty is concentration on our common heritage.*

The Council is setting an example. For the greater part, the *Decree on Ecumenism* emphasizes the things which unite us before God. Our common heritage is indeed great. As to the Orthodox Churches, there is a common deposit of faith and worship of God. It is surprising that, in view of such a communion of faith, hope and worship, theologians and churchmen could focus their attention so one-sidedly, if not exclusively, on the few issues separating us. The age of controversial theology, which likewise exerted its unfavorable influence on the various theological schools within the Church, ended with the opening of the Second Vatican Council. The outcome and resulting changes are gratifying.

Young people of today look with suspicion on those few isolated theologians who insist on continuing the old controversial route. They, like lepers, shout with hollow voices from graves and burial vaults, while in their own opinion they are the "holy few." Their mere presence among us is sufficient reason for further penance to all Catholics. All ecumenically minded Catholics must clearly disavow all attitudes of controversy. They furthermore must cultivate the ecumenical style of dialogue when talking to these extreme conservatives. By our sincere efforts to gather the "red-hot coals" of our carefully collected energies of understanding love to spread on their heads (in their behalf), shall be prepared for a more effective ecumenical dialogue not only with those friendly and open-minded, but also with those less receptive brothers and sisters among the various Christian communities still separated from us.

In my own experience I have found it most distressing to listen to the petty complaints of some Monsignor who does not wish to accept the ecumenically minded and more humble Church of the Second Vatican Council as the Church of his choice. Similarly, I feel greater frustration when I am attacked by certain canonists who launch their attack from the well-protected battlements of their casuistry and hurl their accusations against various Protestant denominations and ecumenically minded theologians and bishops, than when I am subjected to unpleasant opposition from men and women of other Churches. One might ask the question whether there is greater openness among our Protestant and Orthodox brethren than among certain Catholic circles. We understand the deeply felt solidarity between the complaining Monsignor and the Catholic canonist, entrenched behind the letter of the law. Their common problem should remind us of our own short-comings.

2. *Differences of perspectives and expression are not separating walls but mutually enriching factors.*

Shortly before the beginning of the Second Vatican Council a famous ultraconservative archbishop of the Curia postulated that the foremost prerequisite for unity would be the acceptance of Thomistic philosophy as the sole philosophy of the Catholic Church. His syllogism was: If Thomism is true for the Dominicans, it must also be true for the Franciscans. If it is true for the West, it must also be true for the East. If it was true in the 13th century, then it must be equally true throughout all the centuries to follow. The fault of his reasoning lies in the premise

where "being true" is confused with "*the* truth"! Thomas
Aquinas, together with his famous school, is not synonymous with *the* truth! He made a more or less successful
attempt to answer in medieval language the philosophical
questions of his own time. He is praiseworthy for his readiness to enter a dialogue with the religious currents of his
age. He is classical because he was successful in drawing up
formulations which even today vitally enrich our thinking.

The Council clearly dissociated itself from the idea that
one theological or philosophical school should ever have a
monopoly in the Church. Moreover, the Roman Catholic
Church of the West, in her entire historical structure, steers
away from such a monopoly in theological matters. Catholic
unity means multiplicity. "Far from being an obstacle to
the Church's unity, ... diversity of customs and observ-
ances only adds to her comeliness. ... To remove any
shadow of doubt, then, this sacred Synod solemnly declares
that the Churches of the East, while keeping in mind the
necessary unity of the whole Church, have the power to
govern themselves according to their own disciplines, since
these are better suited to the temperament of their faithful.
... Although it has not always been honored, the strict
observance of this traditional principle is among the prerequisites for any restoration of unity. ... What has already
been said about legitimate variety we are pleased to apply
to differences in theological expression of doctrine" (*Decree
on Ecumenism,* Art. 16, 17).

3. *Fruitful dialogue presupposes willingness to listen and
to learn.*

The response from a leading voice in the conservative
opposition at the Council to a brotherly invitation for
dialogue in controversial issues was: "Do not expect me
to enter into a dialogue in which I am expected to change

something of what I am and what, in full allegiance to the will of God, I consider right."

It is understood that the Catholic Church in its ecumenical dialogue must neither deny its own identity, nor renounce its fidelity to God. Nevertheless, the Church must make a distinction between the things of God, that is, faithfulness to Divine Revelation and obedience to the divine will, on the one hand, and on the other, the things which are prone to error as we search for God or are simply expressions of human weakness, limitation and sin. The Church would indeed deny its identity if she had no desire to rectify or to reform anything.

In a similar manner, as the theological schools within the Church are interdependent in their effort to safeguard Christian principles and prevent narrowness and one-sidedness, so also the partners in the ecumenical dialogue will mutually gain through their exchange of opinion. The Church will always hold to matters of revealed truth. Yet the ecumenical dialogue can help to express such truths in more intelligible ways and thereby aid the incorporation of these truths into the total view of faith and way of life. Humility, love of truth, and the willingness to learn should not only characterize the life of the individual theologian but also the entire Church as a community of salvation and faith.

The willingness and ability to listen and to learn is a decisive criterion of a truly "spiritual man." However, false conciliatory approaches, referred to as irenicism, must be avoided because they are harmful to the Catholic doctrine and obscure its genuine meaning (Cf *Decree on Ecumenism,* Art. 11).

Catholics, in their ecumenical dialogue, will particularly guard those truths of our common heritage which have not only been preserved faithfully but even developed with special care by our non-Catholic partners. Furthermore, when explaining certain typical aspects of Catholic doctrine, we should "remember that in Catholic teaching there exists an order or "hierarchy" of truths, since they vary in their relationship to the foundation of the Christian faith" (*Decree on Ecumenism*, Art. 11). At the same time, "Catholic belief needs to be explained more profoundly and precisely, in ways and in terminology which our separated brethren can readily understand" (*Decree on Ecumenism*, Art. 11). Mutual patience and assistance among the Christian partners is a primary prerequisite for ecumenical dialogue. Our chief aim should be to make the Christian message more intelligible and understandable to modern man who is tempted by disbelief, or has fallen prey to atheism.

4. *The ecumenical dialogue must penetrate the entire Church.*

The "ecumenical movement" requires thoughtful preparation. In our efforts toward Christian unity, we must recognize our limitations. Even the most learned theologian will realize his limitations in competence because at times it is difficult to make clear distinctions and decisions. Knowledge, wisdom and humility usually go hand in hand.

Although the ecumenical dialogue between expert theologians of the different Churches and ecclesial communities is most important, every Christian has his share of responsibility in the ecumenical movement, that is, in fostering of unity among Christians. To accomplish this goal, the Council stipulates that the theological instructions for future shepherds and priests "must be presented from an ecumenical point of view" (*Decree on Ecumenism*, Art. 10). The decree then continues to give the reason for the above injunction by saying: "so that at every point they may more accurately correspond with the facts of the case."

The *Decree on Priestly Formation* declares: "According to an opportune evaluation of the conditions of various regions, students should be led to a more adequate understanding of the Churches and ecclesial communities separated from the Roman, Apostolic See. Thus the students can contribute to the restoration of unity among all Christians according to the directives of this sacred Synod" (*Decree on Priestly Formation*, Art. 16). Recently, outstanding theology departments at Protestant-affiliated universities, in their desire for true ecumenical dialogue, have erected chairs for Catholic theologians. The author of these essays is fortunate to hold such chairs as visiting professor in three Protestant university departments.

Ecumenical Movement

As soon as ecumenical dialogue is established in which mutual respect and understanding predominates, Christians from different ecclesial communities will discover a considerable common heritage. In such dialogue they can jointly testify to a faith and to a hope that will not come to nought. Christian hope bears special witness in active love. "Since in our times cooperation in social matters is very widely practiced, all men without exception are summoned to united effort. Those who believe in God have stronger summons, but the strongest claims are laid on Christians, since they have been sealed with the name of Christ. Cooperation among all Christians vividly expresses that bond which already unites them, and it sets in clearer relief the features of Christ the Servant. . . . Through such cooperation, all believers in Christ are able to learn easily how they can understand each other better and esteem each other more, and how the road to the unity of Christians may be made smooth" (*Decree on Ecumenism*, Art.

12). The *Pastoral Constitution on the Church in the Modern World* similarly expresses this hope of cooperation for the benefit of all of mankind (Cf *Pastoral Constitution on the Church in the Modern World*, esp. Art. 89ff).

Common Prayer for Unity

The ecumenical movement is founded on the will of God as expressed in the farewell prayer of Jesus addressed to His disciples. The chief causes of separation are human weakness and sin. True contrition, which prepares the hearts for reunion, is a gift of God's grace. All the endeavors for unity should be penetrated by the conviction of man's weakness and the power of God's grace. This confident desire for ultimate unity finds fitting expression in prayer, as well as in an action, purified and strengthened by prayer. Hence it should be normal and logical that Christians from different communities try to gather for joint prayer services, especially those for unity. The Council expresses caution and a certain restraint because this is an entirely new territory for most Catholics. "In certain special circumstances, such as in prayer services 'for unity' and during ecumenical gatherings, it is allowable, indeed, desirable, that Catholics should join in prayer with their separated brethren. Such prayers in common are certainly a very effective means of petitioning for the grace of unity, and they are a genuine expression of the ties which even now bind Catholics to their separated brethren. 'For where two or three are gathered together for my sake, there am I in the midst of them' " (Mt 18:20) (*Decree on Ecumenism*, Art. 8).

Our goal is worship in the fullness of community, namely, a common celebration of the Eucharist as the expression of unity in the one and only Church (Cf *Decree* on *Ecumenism,* Art. 4). One of the fundamental questions of ecumenism which arises today is: In what sense is the Eucharist a symbol of unity? Is it a static symbol of an already achieved unity or is it a dynamic sign of the powerful work of God to guide us in our decisive steps— a sign of our willingness, with God's grace, to contribute our share toward the achievement of this goal? The Council offers at least a practical hint for our guidance in the future: Although the ecclesial union with the Orthodox Churches has as yet not been fully achieved, the Council considers the possibility (even before mutual retraction of bulls of excommunication) of a certain worship in common, including the celebration of the Eucharist. This is not "merely possible, but is recommended" with the approval of the Church (Cf *Decree on Ecumenism,* Art. 15; Cf *Decree on Eastern Catholic Churches,* Art. 27).

The Eucharist is a symbol of unity. In order that its significance be more fully realized in a concelebrated liturgy, we need a certain degree of unity, although not unity at every point; for perfect unity as a reality can be realized only in heaven where all danger of discord has ceased. Careful theological work and prudent pastoral guidance by the hierarchy is required so that optimum requirements for common worship can be agreed upon. As the Christian communities draw closer in true ecumenical endeavors, this aspect needs constant reevaluation. It is self-evident that outdated rules, found in handbooks of morality and formulated in a time of unecumenical thinking and striving, must be replaced with new ecumenical thinking.

CHAPTER SEVENTEEN

Blessed Are the Peacemakers

The messianic hope of God's people in the Old Testament can be summarized in one word: Peace. The resurrected Christ offers His Apostles peace as His greeting and gift. He sends them out as messengers of messianic peace. The Law of the New Covenant praises the children of peace, those who receive peace from the Lord and who make peace, those who carry peace in their hearts and negotiate peace (Cf Mt 5:9). They are the true sons and daughters of God.

With this in mind, some clear distinctions must be made. The messianic expectation, as expressed in many utterances of the apostles before Pentecost, was too much an expectation of a purely earthly kingdom of power and peace. At the other extreme were those pietists who could be found in almost any community, pietists concerned only with their own peace of mind and who felt no challenge, on the basis of this, to spread peace among men. The "peace of the Lord" is neither of these.

Messianic peace is a gift that comes to life in the heart of the disciple of Christ in the midst of what may be a rather stormy life. It is a reality that extends far beyond the vicissitudes of this life. The true disciple of Christ is rooted firmly in his faith and in his hope for this messianic peace even when the world is torn with dissension and war. Messianic peace is a fruit of the Holy Spirit, a gift from above which can only be asked and received in humility. But where this fruit of the Spirit is truly received, there

G

it will bear fruit; it will radiate peace. One cannot be a son or daughter of God without promoting peace in one's own world, one's environment, and to the extent of one's own abilities. A Christian's acceptance of the message of peace is indivisible.

Christ, the Prince of Peace

"That earthly peace which arises from the love of neighbor symbolizes and results from the peace of Christ who comes forth from God the Father. For by His cross the Incarnate Son, the Prince of Peace, reconciled all men with God. By thus restoring the unity of all men in one people and one body, He slew hatred in His own flesh. After being lifted on high by His resurrection, He poured the Spirit of love into the hearts of men" (*Pastoral Constitution on the Church in the Modern World*, Art. 78).

The great peace program with which the last document of the Second Vatican Council concludes is built around the commitment to Christ as the Prince of Peace. Unless my eyes deceive me, the future of the world and largely of Christianity also, will be decided by whether all men of good will are going to cooperate energetically in making this program work. An examination of conscience about the contribution to peace on all levels cannot be absent from any Christian catechism of the future.

Our Christian mission in regard to peace on earth must begin with the endeavor to know Christ better, the Prince of Peace. His coming to earth is a message of peace to all men of good will, to all men through whom the gracious kindness of God is revealed. It is a message which, first, reaches the poor (Cf Lk 2:8-20). Christ's messianic office means a particular proximity to the poor and oppressed. He has come to "set the downtrodden free, to proclaim the Lord's year of favor" (Lk 4:18-19). Christ did not come to be judge over matters of law. But He brings peace on every level wherever His message finds acceptance. "He will ... turn the hearts of fathers toward their children and the disobedient back to the wisdom that the virtuous have, preparing for the Lord a people fit for him" (Lk 1:17).

Concord and union among His disciples are a sign of Christ's presence among them. He sends forth His disciples to announce and to bring peace to every house: so much so that the Apostle of the Peoples can say, "He is the peace between us" (Eph 2:14). This he says with reference to the calling of all people and all men to the kingdom of Peace. The new people of God must recognize no wall between Jews and pagans. He made peace "through the cross to unite them both in a single Body and reconcile them with God. In His own person He killed hostility" (Eph 2:15). When the disciples accept the gift and the calling of all-embracing love from the Lord, then the blessing of Col 3:15 is directed to them: "May the peace of Christ reign in your hearts, because it is for this that you were called together as parts of *one* body."

The Message of Peace and the Courage of Division

The peace message of Christ must not be belittled. It must be envisioned with all its heights, depths, and tensions. Jesus tells His disciples, "Peace I bequeath you, my own peace I give you, a peace the world cannot give, this is my gift to you" (Jn 14:27). However, he who desires the peace of Christ must follow Him in the decisive "no" to any form of unsound peace. This is expressed with utmost urgency in the word: "Do you suppose that I am here to bring peace on earth? No, I tell you, but rather division" (Lk 12:51).

Just as Jesus Himself became a nuisance to the Pharisees and scribes and just as He took the consequences upon Himself, the disciple, too, must persevere in his mission to bring peace, even though it might bring him disgrace and suffering. The best test of the messianic peacemaker lies in his love for his enemies. "Alas for you when the world speaks well of you! This was the way their ancestors treated the false prophets. But I say this to you who are listening: Love your enemies, do good to those who hate you, bless those who curse you, pray for those who treat you badly" (Lk 6:26-28). These central words of the Sermon on the Mount show the strength and the power of messianic peace. The disciple of Christ whose heart is filled with the peace of Christ cannot be embittered by anything. The concentrated power of love that embodies and announces the messianic peace, proves its worth in the attitude of genuine non-violence. Yet this must not be interpreted as mere abstention from violent measures. Only that inner strength is decisive that overcomes evil by doing good.

Temptation will forever exist in the desire to dissolve the polarity—one might almost say the contrasting harmony—in favor of the one pole. A wrong irenism will deny the testimony to the truth—be it "peace" with those in power in one's own Church or peace with the currents of the day—while infuriated fanatics would force a victory for truth with the help of the stake. The one pays for his peace with indifferentism to truth and love. The one becomes a pacifist because of apathy and timidity in the cause of justice, the other is willing to defend the just cause, as he sees it, with every possible means, even to the point where none of those who were in need of justice will survive in the end.

The disciple of Christ can fight the battle for His true peace only with the weapon of love. He who wants to fight at the forefront of peace must be well equipped with love and the strength of the peace of Christ. He who wants to spread and establish peace among men must be ready to pay its price. An easy pacifism has nothing in common with the gospel. To those, however, who are quick with their sword, it is said: "Put your sword back, for all who draw the sword will die by the sword" (Mt 26:52). Neither the spiritual nor the worldly sword furthers the cause of Christ and of peace among men when enthusiasm for justice is not matched with the persevering strength of a love that endures and hopes everything.

Dialectical materialism breaks up the synthesis of the desired peace into a thesis and antithesis of hatred and struggle. A redemption of Marxism will be possible only if we Christians succeed in making credible, with great love and with the willingness to make sacrifices, the synthesis of courageous sacrifices for truth and justice and a love that overcomes every obstacle.

Indivisibility of Peace

Christ is not only the redeemer of souls; He is the redeemer and Lord of the world. The truly redeemed, those who accept the gift of redemption with an undivided heart and with all their faith, become messengers of and witnesses to peace on all levels and in all the different areas of life.

Ecumenism is an acceptance of Christ's commandment to make peace. Christians must bury their swords in their search for the full truth of Christ, if they want to draw nearer to the truth of God and if they want to become credible heralds of the peace of Christ among all nations. The feud between different schools of theologians which has done much damage to truth and salvation must not be supplanted by even fiercer feuds between the progressives and conservatives. The existence of different schools is justified only if it is an expression of a common search, a dialogue in love, and unity in diversity. Very different degrees of progressivism and concern for the preservation of a precious heritage do no harm to the Church if everyone concerned endures in his testimony to the messianic peace, not only in spite of but actually because of the presence of diversity.

Concern for the peace of Christ must particularly characterize marriage and family life. Relatives and neighbors, one's job, the relationship between employer and employee, union and entrepreneur, parties and nations are all realms wherein the messianic peace of Christ should be reflected through the efforts and testimony of Christian men and women. No area must be left out, for everything is created, redeemed and directed toward Him who is called the Prince of Peace. Messianic peace does not shelter us in a glass house; rather it sends us forth into the world, frequently to the most stormy places in the world. A Christian must never be entangled in the hatred of the world. Yet he must be "entangled," that is committed to the struggle of mankind for peace and justice.

Not all men can do everything. Each one of us is called upon to serve such undivided peace with his talents and in his place. One person has the charism to further peace in the ecclesial realm, in his parish, in his order, or in his diocese, between liberals and conservatives, between clergy and laymen. However, he will never seek a peace that would shut the doors, for instance, to ecumenism, the peace of all Christianity. He will not be able to achieve peace for the price of an officially ordered disinterest for social justice or of a betrayal of the integration of the discriminated. Another person will have the charism to stand up against narrow-mindedness and fanatical intolerance among the ranks of his own Church or his own party. Yet he cannot be sure of his charism unless he possesses a good amount of humor and unless he knows how to combine a word of reconciliation with a gentle "nudge in the ribs." Whoever lacks humor might better look for another field and another object for his pacification efforts.

Everyone who has something to do with the business world must contribute somehow to social peace. Everyone who is eligible to vote can somehow serve the cause of justice and peace with his ballot. Those who have a charism for making peace, because of the gifts of God and of their position, must become heralds of mutual understanding, of justice in mutual respect. The professional politician has a special calling to serve the peace between parties, interest groups and nations. A Christian who has all the necessary qualifications for a political career will not say, "I might soil my hands." Rather, he will gratefully welcome such an extraordinary opportunity to serve the cause of peace in his world and in his time. Journalist, editor, and commentator also have special responsibilities in the matter of social and international peace, for whether nations will come closer and whether politicians will be forced to think thoughts of peace depends greatly upon public opinion, the formation of which these people can effectively influence. There is no one who cannot make his modest yet indispensable contribution to peace, if only through his respectful attitude toward other nations and members of other races and religions.

The Theory of the Just War

The history of Christianity shows, besides the great prophets of messianic peace, also men of the sword. These Christians range from those enthusiastic crusaders who took the sack of Constantinople upon their consciences, to a Francis of Assisi who called on the Sultan with the gospel of love as his sole weapon. Among the theologians there were great heralds of peace as well as patient defenders of the just war. But the conditions and the theory of the "just war" cannot be lumped together indiscriminately, as was frequently the case in the past. The conditions for a "just war" were worked out so penetratingly by some theologians that a conscientious Christian who trusted those theologians lost all desire to volunteer for military service. Those conditions for a just war were meant to curb the military ambitions of the princes. Frequently it was the most feasible method of checking war in the historical situation. Yet it cannot be denied that other moralists did not weigh the conditions for a "just war" too carefully. There were almost always princes of the Church on both sides who were all too eager to bless weapons and armies and to curse those of the other side.

Pope John XXIII, in his encyclical *Pacem in terris* (Peace on Earth), and the Second Vatican Council, in its chapter on the "Fostering of Peace and the Promotion of a Community of Nations," continue in the tradition of those theologians and heralds of peace who drew up so many conditions to the possibility of a just war that a justification of war became close to impossible. The following sentence ought to be understood with this in mind: "Certainly, war has not been rooted out of human affairs. As long as the danger of war remains and there is no competent and sufficiently powerful authority at the international level, governments cannot be denied the right to legitimate defense, once every means of peaceful settlement has been exhausted" (*Pastoral Constitution on the Church in the Modern World*, Art. 79). One must not, by any means, take this sentence apart from the rather sharp condemnation of any form of total war, any war of aggression, or any meaningless defensive war.

However, the Second Vatican Council does not limit itself at all to stipulating more up-to-date conditions for a just war. It praises those who "renounce the use of violence in the vindication of their rights" (*Pastoral Constitution on the Church in the Modern World*, Art 78). The Council unmasks the threat of war as a consequence of man's sinfulness and it announces the hope for peace as the fruit of conversion: "But to the extent that men vanquish sin by a union of love, they will vanquish violence as well, and make these words come true: 'They shall beat their swords into plowshares and their spears into pruning hooks; one nation shall not raise the sword against another, nor shall they train for war again'" (Is 2:14) (*Pastoral Constitution on the Church in the Modern World*, Art. 78).

The Council is definitely aware of the intricacy of the situation, yet it makes clear to everyone that the situation is infinitely serious. It is possible that mankind is already close to ridding itself of this maniac belief that wars are necessary. "Divine Providence urgently demands of us that we free ourselves from the age-old slavery of war. But if we refuse to make this effort, we do not know where the evil road we have ventured upon will lead us" (*Pastoral Constitution on the Church in the Modern World*, Art. 81).

Some pacifists were disappointed by the texts of the

Council. They expected a clear, unequivocal condemnation of any form of war. They clamored for the loudest trumpets of justice and judgment. However, the critics overlook the fact that the Council did not limit itself to speaking against war. Its decisive message is that it points out the way to peace. Yet this demands much more of every individual and of all nations than a comfortable pacifism that is satisfied with a mere condemnation of war. He who wants peace must pool his energies with the common efforts for peace.

The untiring sermons for peace and the peace efforts of Pope Paul are completely in line with the peace program of the Council. The establishment of a special secretariat for the fostering of justice and peace is a promising beginning that lets us hope that more and more Christians will realize how messianic peace, the salvation promised to us by Christ, demands a new attitude and steady efforts for peace on all levels.

The upbringing of our youth and the education of adults must focus on all the implications of the Christian peace mission. It must be universally realized how absurd it is to speak either of a "just war" or of absolute pacifism when the furthering of social peace, of justice, and friendship among nations is not given due attention, and when the necessary sacrifices for the peaceful settlement, order and reconciliation of all nations are not made.

CHAPTER EIGHTEEN

Man—the Product or the Shaper of His Environment?

It was the conviction of Karl Marx that human civilization, including morality and religion, is a product and a super-structure of the given economic conditions. He claimed that the economic environment shaped man. The one-sidedness of this view has repeatedly been exposed. Yet it is tragic that the Christianity of the last century replied to this mainly with apologetics and with the opposite kind of one-sidedness. The only proper answer is the humane trans-formation of economic and social relationships together with a free commitment to those values which exceed by far the mere economic realm. Thereby it is essential that we realize how the entire constitution of our environment influences the individual and the group, the extent to which and the way in which we are responsible for our environment.

Sin and Redemption in An Environmental Perspective

The picture of the garden of paradise which had been entrusted to man for cultivation and the other picture of man's expulsion from this garden into a new environment that is spiked with thorns and thistles and cursed with man's lust for power—to use the terminology of those days—speaks distinctly of the cosmic, that is, the environ-mental character of sin. The "sin of the world" is the common entanglement in sin of men enveloped in their own ego, an entanglement which is represented by and continued in the human environment. Thus created things, the environment which had been created for man became subject to frustration and corruption, not of their own doing, but because of man's sinful, free decision. The proliferating thorns and thistles on the field of the incompetent farmer are a symbol of a spreading lust for power, selfishness, cowardice, dishonesty, group egoism, and the laziness of those who could rank among the elite of mankind.

Just as sin, and infinitely more so than sin, redemption in Jesus Christ embraces the entire man—man in his environment and with respect to his responsibility for the humane shaping of his environment. Christ radiates peace, happiness, goodness, and mercy over His environment; but He also unmasks the stuffy air surrounding the Pharisees and scribes. Even nature herself obeys Him and serves the message of His love. Nature trembles and protests at the crime committed against Him. All this is an expression of the environmental and cosmic dimension of sin and redemption. Conversion certainly demands first of all a new attitude, a change of heart and of its innermost desires. But the new attitude can neither be genuine nor lasting unless it also finds expression in a new relationship to the entire environment. Those who have received the downpayment on the new freedom of the sons and daughters of God are perceptive to the groans of everything created and its yearning to be free from frustration and corruption in order to enjoy the freedom of the children of God (Cf Rom 8:21).

It is not true that man is a mere product of his environment. The environment is ultimately that which man has made out of the good creation of God. Environment has its human history, the history of men who have molded their environment, be it good or bad, of men who neglected to shape it in conformity to their calling and the dignity of man. Environment is the investment of either responsible freedom and love or irresponsible selfishness and lust for power. The environment is in many respects the field where the lazy servant hid his talent. That is why he becomes a product of his environment.

The environment is the field where the eschatological battle between the sons of light and the powers of darkness is taking place. There we have to face in battle: "the Sovereignties and the Powers who originate the darkness in this world, the spiritual army of evil in the air" (Cf Eph 6:10-20) in the very atmosphere surrounding us. We have to do infinitely more than merely exorcise these thunderous forces. A Christian musters all his energies to make his environment a dwelling place for the message of the gospel; he must drive out the evil spirits of lying, slyness, inordinate ambition, laziness and cowardice. "So stand your ground, with truth buckled round your waist, and integrity for a breastplate, wearing for shoes on your feet an eagerness to spread the gospel of peace and always carrying the shield of faith so that you can use it to put out the burning arrows of the evil one. And then you must accept salvation from God to be your helmet and receive the word of God from the Spirit to use as a sword" (Eph 6:14-17).

The environmental aspect of sin and redemption can be translated into the following basic rule of Christian decision-making: No one can save himself from the solidarity of evil in Adam and from the enslaving power of his unenlightened environment unless he totally surrenders himself to solidarity in Christ and works on the recuperation and humanization of his environment as best he can. This total perspective of salvation also includes a fact known to the secular man: the less one labors for a reasonable transformation of an environment mindful of the well-being of all, the more one turns into a product of unfavorable environmental influences. Man will be less the product of his environment as he conducts himself more vigilantly and more responsibly in his confrontation with it. However, since the environment is a result of the freedom or the absence thereof on the part of so many people, a responsible attitude toward the environment calls for solidarity and cooperation with all men of good will.

What constitutes the environment where division and decision take place? It is made up of the men with whom we come into direct or indirect contact. It is our cultural heritage, the world in which we live, civilized nature, the conditions of economic and professional life with its organizations and groupings, the complex reality of the political life and legislation, of off-time entertainment, particularly however, of public opinion which approaches us through thousands of channels.

Gratitude as Basic Attitude

The pessimist idles his time away with complaints about the sad shape of his environment. A moralist who focuses all his attention on the unredeemed state of mankind pictures the environment mainly as an opportunity for sin. The belief in creation and redemption, however, always seeks and discovers primarily the wonders of the Creator and the fruits of redemption. The pessimist pays tribute mainly to the devil. Thus he literally bedevils his environment.

Not everybody is in an equally fortunate position of having been exposed to a rich cultural heritage in his own family and his more immediate environment. But somehow everyone takes part in the treasures of human civilization.

Gratitude opens one's eyes for the "one talent" or for the five talents which are held before us by our environment. Only he who is grateful will succeed in truly acquiring all the good things in his environment for the benefit of his own personal enrichment. Gratitude makes a man desirous and capable of keeping goodness alive in the environment, of purifying it and passing it on in new frequently better forms.

Scientific agriculture and modern industry are founded on the efforts and inventions of millenia of human history. A standstill is not permissible if mankind wants to pursue its course of growth. We find a similar situation in the other numerous aspects of man's total environment. The command, "Conquer the earth" does not apply to the soil alone. Our material, social, cultural and spiritual environment is the gift of our Creator, the gift of the many generations preceding us. We are to pass it on in new form to future generations. Thus, our milieu is the place of our responsibility to ourselves, to our neighbor and to those who come after us.

For instance, if we understand how much we owe to the political order, then this precisely will be a challenge to help us in removing political grievances, in strengthening and developing all the assets of our different political communities. If the liturgy and other forms of piety in our Church have made us gifts, then we will also know that the community has a right to our own personal contribution in terms of a better performance of liturgy and the forms of piety in Church and family.

Immunization or, Curse?

A Christian, on the other hand, cannot afford to be blind to the negative aspects and dangers impinging upon him in his environment. One's sleepiness and a naive optimism could well stab him in the back. The vigilant Christian faces reality in all its complexity. The first thing that thereby comes to his mind is not flight but loving responsibility, a healing and helping influence in cooperation with all those who are willing and capable of the same.

The saying, "to the pure all things are pure" simplifies the problem unduly. We are all in the pilgrim condition. Although we have taken up sides with Christ in a most serious commitment, we nevertheless have not yet completely driven out our Adamitic thoughts and desires. All that is wrong in our environment has secret allies within us. That is why our encounter with our environment requires a critical attitude toward ourselves as well as our environment. Somehow we must be aware of the limits of our vulnerability. Vigilance is always called for. But the great healing power, the true immunization against most dangers stemming from our environment is a loving attitude of active responsibility.

The Christian in the world of today must have a deep concern for the study of his environment. He must see how the environment influences the freedom of many people. He must learn the difficult art of taking reality seriously and shaping it gradually. Observation and the art of cooperation are thereby indispensable.

He who clearly realizes how much moral and religious development depends on the conditions of the entire environment, and as soon as he discovers that he, too, can make a contribution to the improvement of the environment, he will not be challenged by the anxious search for self-preservation and self-fulfillment only, but above all, the loving concern and responsibility for his neighbor will summon all his energies in a way not likely to imperil his own identity unnecessarily.

Where nothing or little can be changed, there will frequently be good reasons to look for a different environment, for instance in a different neighborhood, at a different job, in a different parish. Perhaps one will retreat for a while from a certain milieu to gain a firmer footing though a more lively community. For instance, he who belongs to a parish where the liturgy and the sermons are more like the "God is dead" bit than the announcement of the mysteries of Easter, and who realizes how his own faith becomes less and less lively because of all this sterile mechanism, will do his best in searching for a community that will make him and his family enjoy his faith again. One will be all the more capable of exercising a healthy influence on the worldly milieu the more one finds the support of a lively ecclesial milieu, at least of a small group of Christians happy in the faith.

The Power of Public Opinion

Among all the influences of environment, public opinion deserves particular attention today. It had at all times a great impact on the average man. Yet today, it has become particularly eloquent due to the modern mass media of press, film, radio and television. Their transmitters reach into even the most remote village. We have become more dependent on public opinion than we can ever imagine. We owe much to it, but we are also very vulnerable because of it; this is all the more true where we fail actively to participate in the shaping of this very public opinion. A public opinion is healthy insofar as many people are able to distinguish between established truths and debatable opinions, between reasonably proved common convictions and collective biases. Furthermore, much depends on how a joint and publicly avowed struggle for well-founded

H

opinions can be set off against maneuvers of pressure groups.

These basic rules for a healthy formation of opinion are particularly valid in the realm of the ecclesial community. On February 17, 1950, in a significant address to the world as well as to the Church, Pope Pius XII emphasized the necessity of a healthy formation of public opinion. "Those who do not know or only barely know the Catholic Church will be surprised to hear this. For she, too, is a living organism. And something would be missing from its life if it lacked public opinion, a lack for which the shepherds and the faithful would have to take the blame." The Second Vatican Council underscored the impact of public opinion. Thereby free speech is particularly assured; however, care must be taken to distinguish between that which is a definite deposit of faith and that which is left open to inquiry. Such care is a particular concern.

The Council clearly realized that theology can neither serve the penetration and promulgation of the truth of the faith nor can it remain in touch with life itself unless theologians are permitted their necessary freedom. "In order that such persons may fulfill their proper function, let it be recognized that all the faithful, clerical and lay, possess a lawful freedom of inquiry and of thought, and the freedom to express their minds humbly and courageously about those matters in which they enjoy competence" (*Pastoral Constitution on the Church in the Modern World*, Art. 62). The Church should definitely be the model for a responsible and honest formation of opinion in the spirit of Christian freedom.

In a rapidly changing world there is need for a joint effort in Church and society to come to a clear assessment of the situation and the best possible ways for a solution.

In many instances public authority must decide one way or another. However, it will steer askew the modern mentality if it fails to communicate the necessary insights to a large following even if it has to admit its limitations. This is even more important for the ecclesial milieu than for the secular. Respect for truth as well as concern for mature obedience requires, in many situations, that problems which cannot be solved with one clear insight be recognized as open questions without hesitation. The last guarantee which the Church can give with regard to revealed truth prohibits the confusing of isms or personal pious concepts with doctrines of faith.

"The Christian method wants to convince with nobility in objective presentation; it desires to persuade with reasons and not with suggestive pressure" (Pope John in an Address on December 4, 1960). The realization of the limits of one's own insight and knowledge will have to join forces with tact and respect for one's partner in a conversation. Healthy differences of opinion will always be a welcome and ever new reason for all to search more deeply, to inform themselves more thoroughly, and to stay away from a wrong kind of security.

In view of the presentations by the mass media, a modern Christian must endeavor more than ever to select and discern critically. This is the very purpose of discussions among friends about the things one heard or saw. According to the measure of his own judgment, the vigilant Christian will also display his acknowledgment, agreement or critical rejection when confronted with journalists and institutions that select programs and publications.

CHAPTER NINETEEN

Witnesses to Truth

Christ, personified truth and witness *par excellence* to truth in the world, gave His disciples the exalted mission: "You will receive power when the Holy Spirit comes on you, and then you will be my witnesses not only in Jerusalem but throughout Judaea and Samaria, and indeed to the ends of the earth" (Ac 1:8). The whole-hearted acceptance of this challenge will be the deciding factor in understanding Christian morality and existence. The latter must be based on a personal relationship with Christ. Only in Him and through Him will we penetrate to the truth underlying our own existence. This in turn will make our relationship with truth humble and dedicated. Our desire to witness or proclaim Christ must determine our very style of life. An insincere attitude to truth would render the witness both incredible and worthless. Our mission to be witness to truth demands implicit sincerity and credibility in all conceivable walks of life.

Christ: *The Way, the Truth and the Life*

Man as such is not merely confronted with abstract truths and material goods. He is created in the Word of God. Man's innermost being, as well as the magnificence of the entire creation, are manifestations of God, the ultimate source and destination of all being. Man's single-hearted seeking of God is a basic prerequisite for a fuller self-realization and a generous responsiveness to God. Only

thus will he ultimately arrive at the truth underlying hi
existence.

Man's relationship with truth in the last analysis de
pends on his personal confrontation with Christ—tru
God and true man—in an unfaltering faith and a tota
self-surrender, a whole-hearted acceptance of Christ a
truth personified. Christ came into this world to bea
witness to truth. Christ is more than a mere philosophe
teacher or preacher. His entire life radiates truth, namel
the truth that God is love desirous to reveal Himself an
His love for man in His only-begotten Son. Christ, in th
fullest sense of the word, is the truthful witness because H
lay down His life for truth. In turn, the Father, by glorify
ing His Son in the Resurrection, gave proof of Christ'
testimony for the truth.

Christ sent forth His disciples equipped with th
power of the Holy Spirit. With the aid of the Holy Spiri
He tries to fashion His disciples after Himself so that to
gether in Him and with Him they may witness to the trutl
Above all, the Holy Spirit gives life in Christ Jesus. Th
docile disciple of Christ is not confronted with mer
abstractions and principles—his very life is Christ. Thu
all truth becomes life-giving for him. On the other hanc
without an intimate relationship with Christ all truths be
come lifeless, ineffective and even false because only i
Him and in connection with Him they gain their full mear
ing. They are not something parallel with Christ, rathe
they are true and genuine to the extent that they procee
from Christ and lead to Him in the same manner tha
Christ proceeds from the Father and tries to lead all thing
back to the Father.

The disciple of Christ comes to the full realization o
truth only if he is willing to risk his life for the sake o
Christ, just as Christ had given His life in order to lea

us to the fullness of truth in God and to an existence according to truth.

Humble and Sincere Relationship with Truth

The disciple of Christ must approach truth in an attitude of humility. Christ alone may call Himself the truth. We in turn are true only in so far as we receive the light of truth from God which disposes us to a complete self-surrender. Here on earth we perceive truth as through a mirror. Furthermore, since we often make little progress on our way of conversion, the mirror is not without dark and blind spots. A humble man is always aware of shortcomings and therefore admits his mistakes, errors and ignorance. Thus he continuously gains more insight and avoids leading others astray. The intolerant fanatic for truth mistakenly indentifies himself and his imperfect perception of truth with truth itself. He is an adamant opponent to religious freedom, namely, the liberty of every man to seek truth in absolute sincerity and to adhere to it in the measure that he has perceived it. The fanatic for truth draws the sword, raises opposition, and plans intricate measures of pressure of an economic and social nature against all those who do not share his views. He does this with the slogan: "Error has no right to exist." Although error has no right to exist, the fanatic interprets this truth in his own way, namely, that he alone is the possessor of truth. He identifies himself with truth. Whoever differs with his personal views he considers a man in error because he regards himself the sole heir and possessor of truth. In relation to his fellow-man, he confuses error with the one erring even when confronted with an honest quest for truth.

The truth fanatic proves himself not only arrogant in his attempt to force his opinion on others, oftentimes through state and civil legislation, but he likewise proves himself an unbeliever because he does not believe in the power of Christ, namely, the power of the loving witness to truth. The truth fanatic, who persecutes or insults those adhering to other schools of thought or plans of reform, is lacking the passionate love for truth which Christ, the true witness for truth, exemplified. To judge by human standards, Christ disarmed Himself. He spoke the language of love through justice and humility. If the slogan, "Error has no right to exist," were to justify persecution or discrimination, there would be constant war because, due to ignorance more or less culpable, we are all erring in many ways. We are the more credible the more firmly we adhere to Christ and aspire to an ever greater knowledge of Him and His message while we humbly admit the limitations of our own understanding.

It is of the utmost importance for the purity of our faith that we differentiate clearly between articles of faith and mere opinions of various schools of theology, between articles of faith and prudent judgments normally sufficient as guides for prudent behavior. We must be cognizant of the fact that even the most solemn formulations of articles of faith are unable to exhaust the mystery of truth hidden beneath them. Here on earth we shall be unable to arrive at an absolute and final formulation of truth in the sense that we could sit back and enjoy ready made formulae handed down to us. A dogma remains always true if it really is a dogma, namely, a truth revealed by God and authoritatively taught as such by the Church. Yet it remains the pastoral task of the Church to continuously strive towards a deeper penetration of the truth of salvation and to interpret it to all men in a manner intelligible to them. Thereby the various charisms in all Christians should be humbly acknowledged and utilized. A humble love for

ruth itself and for all men to whom truth is to be conveyed
does not permit spiritual idleness.

Our love must bear the characteristics of passionate
zeal as well as deep humility. In his tireless efforts for increased knowledge and a more perfect manner of professing
ruth, the disciple of Christ must be guided not by indifferentism, but by a dedicated love for Christ and the
redeemed. A passionate love for the truth of Christ will
prompt us to be mindful of the fact that love is at the center
of all truth and that truth can be convincingly commu-
nicated only with the meekness of the Master.

Truth and Diplomacy

The efficient diplomat realistically sizes up a situation. Yet,
in every situation his attention centers on ways and means
which best serve his political goals. He thus develops a
particular selective relationship to truth. The truth he
speaks and the truth he hides obviously serve a definite
purpose for him. He makes truth the servant of his goals.
However, this selective relationship with truth will soon
affect not only his words and his reticence, but also his
ability and mode of understanding that soon he will begin
to perceive only those aspects of truth which appear
"useful" to him. None of the apostles of Christ were
schooled in the art of diplomacy. They proclaimed their
message in the simplicity of unselfish witnesses. Today there
is an ever increasing danger for numerous Christians—
not only among the laity but also among priests and
theologians—to resort to diplomacy. The truth of salvation is like the burning bush. Anyone approaching it and
willing to serve it must take off his shoes, walk up to it
with awe and give witness in total unselfishness. The truth
of salvation is not a theory, but rather the transmission of

a life-giving light. It addressed the recipient with an un
selfish love for truth—careful to respect the recipient'
level of comprehension. This sensitive consideration fo
others will be a good guide regarding when to speak and
when to observe silence. Genuine love for the listene
dictates patience in view of the listener's readiness to gras
certain things: "I still have many things to say to you bu
they would be too much for you now" (Jn 16:12). Ther
is a world-wide difference between such considerate dis
cretion and selfish diplomacy. While a calculated relation
ship with truth seeks its own advantages, a considerat
and tactful discretion concerns itself with both the dis
semination of truth and its recipient. A schemer cares fo
truth only in terms of personal advantages. On the othe
hand, the discreet apostle is willing to sacrifice himself fo
truth itself and for those to whom he conveys it.

The most pitiful figure, however, is the so-calle
schemer in Church affairs whose all-embracing goal i
a career. To avoid any confusion, it should be clear that w
are not thinking of the so-called diplomatic service of th
Vatican. We are not referring to those men who serve th
gospel unselfishly and at the same time improve the mutua
understanding among nations without a second thought o
a career or honorary title. Furthermore, the simple chaplain
the religious superior, as well as the theologian, can fa'
prey to the temptation of an insincere relationship to truth
The lay apostle, likewise, must guard against a simila
danger. In addition, certain structures, traditions and cus
toms of the world may increase existing temptations.

Whoever wants to serve the gospel must refrain from
selfish concerns, advantages, or honorary titles. Suc
strivings would disqualify his witnessing power for Chris
and the ability to spread the truth of salvation.

Total Commitment to Sincerity and Truthfulness

Faith is not a special segment or area in the life of the disciple of Christ. No doubt, an article of faith is diametrically different from a scientific precept. Theology proceeds from premises differing from those of mathematics. But the messenger of faith, whether priest or layman, is obligated to truth and mission of witnessing Christ in all his actions. In the long run, it is impossible to maintain an absolutely sincere and unselfish relationship with the world of faith when the character is warped by insincerity and dishonesty or by an all too selfish scheming relationship to fragmentary earthly truths. Either the passionate and humble dedication to the truth of salvation will transform the whole man to absolute truthfulness, or the complacent lack of honesty will extend itself likewise to the religious realm.

Even if despite gross dishonesty in private and public life it were possible to maintain a genuine interest in the truths of faith, such a Christian would simply be unfit for his mission of witnessing Christ. Habitual lies, small dishonesties in business matters, and double dealings in the social and political life, also disqualify a Christian from being a herald of religious truth.

Still more deplorable is the situation if a person attempts to further the cause of the gospel and the Church with small lies or deceptions. At times we may encounter among both priests and laymen the type of person who is more concerned that a Church institution "save its face" than to become a credible witness through an honest admission of truth. If inadvertently an erroneous official statement was made, the credibility of the Church does not suffer, provided that further investigations are made in the light of new knowledge and the error is humbly acknowledged.

In the solemn and world-wide pronouncement of revealed truth, the supreme teaching authority of the Church is infallible. Laymen, priests, bishops, and even popes are fallible or subject to error in quite a few matters. The more conscious they are of this truth, the more willing they will be to admit the mistakes of the past. In the light of new knowledge, they will strive to become more effective witnesses for Christ in firm adherence to the unshakeable articles of faith and in sincere search for a better understanding of truths not defined as articles of faith: "Will you plead God's defense with prevarications?" (Jb 13:7).

Undivided Passion for the Discovery of Truth

The search for the truths of salvation and the acquisition of a deep understanding of Christ are far more important than any thorough training in mathematics. In cases of conflict, the Christian must be willing to decide in favor of the higher values. Yet it would be erroneous to believe that the passionate love for the truths of salvation would diminish or extinguish one's interest in any other pursuit of truth. God is the source of all truth. All things are created in the Word of God and therefore oriented towards Christ. Although faith greatly differs from all worldly knowledge and wisdom, the articles of faith, nevertheless, are not a sector of truth apart from the rest of life. Rather, faith is a light which illumines everything else with its full brightness and its true value. Anyone believing in the redemption of man will also study those truths which will aid him to preserve all human values. The story of salvation gains in eloquence if we grasp the background history of salvation and damnation. The message of the Redeemer of man and the world at large gives added impetus to the study of psychology and the social sciences since they assist us in creating a healthier environment for man and in healing suffering mankind. Modern mathematics and physics are basic prerequisites to meet the needs of a rapidly growing human race. A deeper penetration of all types of truth will prove useful to man, provided the hierarchy of values is not disturbed. Even apart from a practical value, the study of a given science contains a certain fascination for the Christian who recognizes the many rich possibilities which God has placed into His creation. It is a matter of a deeper penetration into the miraculous works of God.

CHAPTER TWENTY

Eschatological
and Timely Virtues

When speaking of virtues we immediately become aware of the discrepancy between virtue in the Greek sense of the word and the prevailing concepts expressed in Holy Scripture. A Stoic's idea of virtue centers on self-preservation, self-control, and self-perfection. For the ancient Greek virtue was synonymous with a man's achievement and fulfillment of existence—not in mere egoism but in sincere acceptance of the cosmic order and a jointly felt responsibility for the common good. Yet, in all this, the chief motive was the concern for the well-being of the ego. Time and again, Christian ethics has attempted to recognize and to accept the true and worthy aspects of this ancient attitude.

The biblical meaning, however, leads us into a different world of ideas. The Greek word for virtue is rarely used in the Bible. Christian morality does not focus its attention on man who is concerned about his own well-being and self-fulfillment, but on God who lovingly invites man to His intimate friendship, on God who calls man, bestows His grace on him, judges him and ultimately saves him from perdition. Man lives in a state of listening and of response. Man's decisions are made in view of the miraculous works of God. The Christian concept of virtue is essentially that of a dialogue, a responsive and worshiping attitude.

There exists a close similarity between the Greek and Chinese concept of virtue, particularly in the emphasis on constancy. Yet, while this constancy chiefly refers to loyalty unto oneself according to classical anthropocentrism, the ethics of the Old and New Covenant rests above all on the faithfulness of God who invites His people to reciprocate His own faithfulness. Constancy has its origin in the grace of God, in the continuity of His saving work. This provides the basis for an even more urgent duty to fidelity. In keeping with the basic attitude of call and response, it is termed *faithfulness*. An unbalanced type of ethics, or one chiefly concerned with "how must I decide in this or that situation," falls short of the reality of the Covenant. The fundamental concept of faithfulness demands an ethics of basic attitudes underlying the ethics of a given decision.

Basic Eschatological Attitudes

Frequently, the word "eschatological" is misinterpreted with a retreat from this present world and an alienation from actual life. Yet this is not the case if we remain faithful to the biblical meaning. Eschatological time signifies the powerful presence of the love of God in the hearts of men, in the midst of a community, and in the fullness of human history. For the Christian, eschatological time signifies the incarnation of the Word of God, the nearness of God, the beginning transformation of human history and human values. Eschatological time means "already begun" but at the same time also "not yet achieved." The very moment we open ourselves to faith, and permit our incorporation into the community of Christ's disciples, we are the sons and daughters of God. At the same time, this reality has still not reached its fulfillment—it is as yet not fully revealed.

Our Christian existence is essentially characterized by

the tension between the "already begun" and the "not yet achieved." This tension absolutely precludes a static presentation of Christian morality. Christian existence is dynamic! The expectation of the end to come confers on the present moment unprecedented urgency. Every routine action, every inflexibility, every self-righteousness and self-reliance must be overcome. A Christian is always "on his way." He has been put on the right path by God Himself.

The eschatological virtues are always timely. However, they are particularly timely in the present hour of salvation which urges so poignantly, which calls for reform, and contains immense opportunities as well as unusual dangers. It is a time which, in all its readiness for change, stands in need of constancy and faithfulness.

All the Christian virtues bear a more or less specifically eschatological character. In the following discussion our attention shall particularly focus on the basic attitudes of hope, faithfulness in vigilance, on the willingness to undergo changes, on patience, and on fortitude and sense of humor.

Christian Hope

Hope is one of the fundamental themes of modern literature. Man lives by hope. The critical days and months of the German army's retreat from Russia and the prison camps showed us how men with the most robust constitutions simply died away while others with much weaker dispositions survived. The difference was in the power of hope. Anyone keeping his hope had a chance to withstand all hardships and privations.

A Christian can be defined as a man of hope. In his faith and in his love he possesses an assurance or guarantee for life eternal. He knows that he is living in a time of immense possibilities for salvation. A Christian is not a pessimist or professional prophet of bad luck; an incorrigible hopelessness is not genuinely Christian. Anyone constantly complaining about "bad times" is an unbeliever, even though he may claim to be a Christian.

Neither is a true Christian a naive optimist who goes into hiding when faced with tensions and disorder proclaiming simply everything as good and in perfect order. Rather, a Christian is an optimist exactly when he is in the midst of tensions and difficulties. The pressure of a new age fill him with patient expectations. He knows that growth is not possible without the concomitants of pain and danger.

A Christian is an optimist in all respects, simply because he puts his trust in God. As a believer, he knows that to those who love God everything will turn into good. He sees that the arm of God is more powerful than the cloven hoof of the Devil.

Christian hope does not permit us to relax on a bed of sloth, bad habits, and old merits. It does not permit us to settle here on earth as if this present time on earth were the only real thing. The Christian is forever reaching for that which lies ahead of him. Ahead of him lies life eternal as well as the great possibilities in the here and now, in today and tomorrow, for an active witness to the belief in life everlasting.

Faithfulness in Vigilance

The basic Christian attitude of faithfulness means anything else but inflexibility, for it has to do with faithfulness in view of the living God, the God of history. In His faithfulness God forever creates anew. He remains the same, yesterday, today, and tomorrow (Cf Hb 13:8). Faithfulness to Him means, therefore, openness to the call of the hour.

Our chief example is Christ Himself in His acceptance of that hour which the Father had prepared for Him. A Christian does not live according to a prefabricated and self-righteous plan. His attitude is rather one of attentiveness and alertness to the present possibilities of salvation in which the energies of the first and final coming of Christ are at work. The grace of Easter, salvation and judgment of the parousia impart new significance to the present moment of grace. That is why it is said: "Wake up from your sleep, rise from the dead, and Christ will shine on you. So be very careful about the sort of lives you lead, like intelligent and not like senseless people. This may be a wicked age, but your lives should redeem it" (Eph 5:14-16). For those who sleep and miss the opportunities prepared by God the days will indeed be wicked.

The monsignor and the old nun who said, "This senile old man (referring to Pope John) might as well have died a couple of years sooner; imagine all the confusion he could have spared us," are representatives of all those to whom and through whom the days become wicked since they do not let themselves be roused from their drowsy routine. Cosmic hours, like the epoch of the Second Vatican Council, leave nobody untouched—they either wake us up and make us more vigilant in our efforts or they expose us in all our weakness. Had the Council not come, many traditionalists could have shouted "obedience, obedience" with a more or less good conscience, while they were merely concerned with their own lethargy. Now they must make up their minds to either show a more enlightened kind of obedience or to refuse being obedient to the advancing

Church in the name of their nightcaps and thereby throw themselves into the adventures of resistance.

Willingness to Change

The time between the first Pentecost and the second coming of Christ is a time of division and decision. The disciples of Christ prove their faithfulness to the Master by their vigilance and willingness to change for the better, by dropping old prejudices and worthless habits. A Christian does not seek the new for the sake of mere change. He does not desire to appear modern at any price. He shuns away from inconstancy and arbitrariness but he also knows that he has not yet arrived at his destination and that, therefore, he still requires a deepening and refining of his attitudes. The life of the individual is a constant conversion, the direction of which is clearly indicated in baptism and explained in the Sermon on the Mount. Should someone believe that he is in no need for change and renewal, he would as yet not even be ready for purgatory. The Church herself is fully aware of the necessity of continuous renewal.

Patience and Fortitude

Often enough during recent months I heard the question: "Will there ever be normal times in the Church again?" In response to the question, "What do you consider normal times?", the answer reveals the desire for times without risks, for an order established once and for all. People of this sort desire a heaven on earth. But their "heaven" is not particularly desirable to men of vital energy; for it resembles more a cemetery than the biblical parables of the Kingdom of heaven. Normal times to the disciple of Christ are those times where there is need for courage to risk things and need for patience. A system of securities is not a sign of the eschatological man, of a man in hope and in the state of grace. The pioneers of the Christian faith were men and women like St. Stephen, the faithful martyr, of whom Scripture briefly reports: "Stephen was filled with grace and power" (Ac 6:8).

The heart of fortitude is perseverance and patience. "Happy those who are persecuted in the cause of right: theirs is the kingdom of heaven" (Mt 5:10). Insults and defamations for the disciples of Christ do not necessarily and always come from pagans and unbelievers. Paul suffered more from unkind brethren, from the traditionalists and career-men, than he suffered from the certainly not tender blows at the hand of pagans.

The genuine disciple of Christ will not be spared sufferings and trials. Patience, together with joy and peace, belongs to the most excellent fruits of the Holy Spirit (Ga 5:22). "My brothers, you will always have your trials, but, when they come, try to treat them as a happy privilege; you understand that your faith is only put to the test to make you patient, but patience too is to have its practical results so that you will become fully-developed, complete, with nothing missing" (Jm 1:2-4).

The Church of today has to go through the anguish of a new epoch. Renewal and the preparation for unity in the Church is not possible without shocks and trials, without self-negation and suffering. Patience includes the courage to make mistakes and not only to admit them humbly, but also to correct them as best we can. A Christian shows patience and perseverance in suffering, in all the vicissitudes of life, in his striving for a genuine renewal, his desire for social reform and for the renewal of the Church. He needs patience with himself as well as patience with others. Yet patience is more than a mere passive virtue. Patience gathers up the energies of love and preserves them for future use. Patience and perseverance prove the power of faith, hope and love.

Equanimity and a Sense of Humor

Under a sky where the gods celebrated their feasts, and settled their arguments far away from men living under the fist of an inescapable fate, the idea of tragedy and a tragical existence developed. Man takes himself seriously but, in return, is not always taken seriously. Unbelieving modern existentialism, which forever is putting its own freedom to the test, describes human existence as nauseating and boring. Camus speaks for many when, in view of the hopeless efforts of Sisyphus, he calls for courage and calmness. He demands a calm and courageous acceptance of life in view of an ultimately exitless (transl. note: Sartre, *No Exit!*) and meaningless existence.

Christian equanimity is of a different nature. In it there is no defiance, nor any hopelessness in misfortune. A Christian possesses equanimity because he firmly believes that in the end love will be victorious over everything else. Through his faith he knows everything will turn into good for those who love God. He projects all his worries onto the Lord. He does all in his power but does not consider himself responsible to turn the wheels of fate. Christian composure has nothing to do with indifference. Rather, it is often the divine peace in a stormy situation, the depth of joy in sadness, courage despite weariness, meekness in the tempest of passions, and self-respect despite humiliation. The equanimity of a Christian signifies the Lord's proximity even when the ship of his life is drifting helplessly amidst a stormy sea. Christians without a sense of humor are living far away from the mountain of beatitudes. Severe criticism, bitter reaction against reformers or traditionalists, the feeling of frustration in resistance are spared only those who, in humility, meekness, charity and patience, put their trust in the Lord.

The disciples of Christ have a sense of humor even though not all of them may have it in the same degree as St. Francis of Assisi and Pope John XXIII. Pope John is reported to have given a fitting reply to a monsignor who was convinced that he had to do everything by himself and who in addition was never satisfied with anything that Pope John did. John XXIII assured the monsignor that he too was tempted by the same worry but that his guardian angel had whispered to him in his sleep: "But Johnny, why do you take yourself so seriously!"

For the sake of the kingdom of God a Christian takes the Kingdom of God and himself seriously but he does not take himself too seriously in his modest spot. He accepts his shadow and at times is able to get a good laugh at himself.

BIBLIOGRAPHY

Lanwer, B. *Die Grundgedanken der Bergpredigt auf dem Hintergrund des AT und des Spätjudentums* (Hiltrup 1934).

Windisch, H. *Der Sinn der Bergpredigt* (Leipzig 1937).

Asmussen, H. *Die Bergpredigt* (Göttingen 1939).

Lindsay, A. D. *The Moral Teaching of Jesus. An Examination of the Sermon on the Mount* (New York 1937).

Soiron, Th. *Die Bergpredigt* (Freiburg 1940).

Stoeger, A. "Ich aber sage euch." *Die Bergpredigt lebendig gemacht* (München 1952).

Dibelius, M. "Die Bergpredigt," *Botschaft und Geschichte. Gesammelte Aufsätze von M. Dibelius* I (Tübingen 1953) 79-174.

Hunter, A. M. *Design for Life. An Exposition of the Sermon on the Mount, its Making, its Exegesis and its Meaning* (London 1953).

Dupont, J. *Les béatitudes. Le problème littéraire. Les deux versions du Sermon sur la montagne e des Béatitudes* (Louvain 1958).

Jeremias, J. *Die Bergpredigt* (Stuttgart 1960).

McArthur, H. K. *Understanding the Sermon on the Mount* (New York 1960).

Davis, W. D. *The Setting of the Sermon on the Mount* (London 1964).

Schmid, J. *Das Evangelium nach Matthäus* (Regensburg 1965).

Gächter, P. *Die literarische Kunst im Matthäusevangelium* (Stuttgart 1965).